War Cries:
Unheard Voices, Unmarked Graves

D1547744

Kerry Arquette

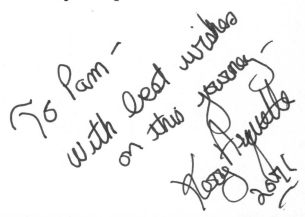

To Pam – with best wishes on this journey – Kerry Arquette 2017

Published by Open Books

Copyright © 2016 by Kerry Arquette

Cover image Copyright © 2016 by Kerry Arquette

ISBN-10: 0997806257
ISBN-13: 978-0997806250

In memory of those lost.
We are listening.

.

Dedicated to the Voices who were brave enough to step forward and who trusted me to tell their stories.

.

Fanny Mina Grotz

There is a place a world away
Where a man may journey after his toils are through.
Without the weight of guilt, or blame, or passion, or pain,
His soul rises like a leaf born on the gentlest breeze.
And as the earth falls below, the air becomes clean and
clear.
Sounds fade to the whirr of a hummingbird's wings.
Odors of life and death dilute, then disappear.

From this ethereal tower that dwarfs the tallest mountain
peaks,
One can view the enormous mosaic of mankind—
From time's conception to the clock's most recent tick.
A man may find his soul space in this scheme,
Gaining perspective on his contribution to the rich and
riotous whole.
And then he will know if his life has been well-lived or
wasted,
And whether, in the end, he was hero or villain.

.

TABLE OF CONTENTS

Fanny Mina Grotz

Setting The Stage   1

Elie Goldberg   5

Ester Kaplan   7

Rachel Stanz   9

Judah Birkowitz   11

Rivka Krylov   13

Kliment Yosselevscka   15

Sarah Anielewicz   17

Jack Fajnzilber   19

Joshua Mahrer   21

Louise Mahrer   23

Vera Zukoski   25

Sonya Reichman   27

Noah Kotmel   29

Odo Wilhelm   31

Grietje Kuilema   33

Lilly Rienks   35

Sonya Griendling	37
Kurt Smolitz	39
Victoria Czastkiewicz	41
Klaus Sichrovsky	43
Niklas Renke	45
Johanna Stine	47
Gerbert Ludwig	49
Herta Kaufmann	51
Jan Kowolski	53
Eva Wilenski	55
Baby Wilenski	57
Astana Kovalov	59
Sonja Rosenberg	61
Resi Hoffmeir	63
Elizabeth Stern	65
Unknown	67
Andre Petit	69
Justified	71
Marina Tereshkova	73

Lola Krantz   75

Adele Opfer   77

Lidia Klimenko   79

Leoind Gerbrandt   81

Golly Sussman   83

The Never-To-Be Born   85

Seymour Poppanick   87

Johann Goldschmitt   89

Renee Robota   91

Werner Mueller   93

Hans Feldman   95

Jacob Baruch   97

Bessie Katz   99

Irony   101

Gossip Mill   103

Stasi Oppenheiner   105

Corporal Thomas Smyth   107

Timothy Robbins   109

Hannah Deutchman   111

Christine Soloman 113

Ivan Romarov 115

Valeriy Romarov 117

Bernard Zahlerova 119

Zarko Jenische 121

Esmerelda Jenische 123

Hilda Wolf 125

Eero Kauranen 127

Kesar Radogost 129

Gustav Moller 131

Thomas Jensen 133

Hana Voigt 135

Chaya Shulamit 137

Rosa Dekel 139

Elsbeth Dekel 141

Hana Rosenmayer 143

Karoline Rosenmayer 145

Alessandro D'Addezio 147

Violette Stein 149

Lia Kumosa   151

Natan Kumosa   153

Tsila Kumosa   155

Saul Markiewicz   157

Juta Benicoeur   159

Itzik Falk   161

Fela Daum   163

Elka Dajbog   165

Margherita Petacci   167

Edda Vittorio   169

Mirek Sectevy   171

Traugott Middlestadt   173

Chorus   175

Sources   177

Acknowledgements   179

Setting the Stage

Germany after WWI was a country in crisis. The harsh terms of the Treaty of Versailles triggered a free fall in the value of the *deutschmark* and led to widespread shortages of staple goods, including food and fuel. Germany's post-war government—the Weimar Republic—foundered, enacting weak and ineffective legislation that failed to check the hyperinflation or address the people's physical and psychological needs. Defeated, demoralized, and despairing, the German people began to turn away from the government and seek out groups with harsher leaders, those who offered a clear message: German strength, solidarity, and a rejection of "non-German" peoples that would return the country to prosperity and dominance.

Despite the government's efforts to check the rising extremism, opposition groups flourished, attracting hundreds of thousands of adherents. Of these, the *Nationalsozialistische Deutsche Arbeiterpartei* (National Socialist German Workers Party) became the most well-known. Colloquially, Germans called the party *Nationalsozialismus* or National Socialism; in English, it has a different name:

The Nazi Party.

Using brutal tactics against opponents and espousing a message of Aryan purity, the Party—and its charismatic leader, Adolf Hitler—rapidly gained power. By 1930, it was Germany's second largest political party; three years later it was the only political party. In 1933, Hitler assumed the country's second-highest office, that of Chancellor. The next year, upon the death of the nation's president, Hitler adopted the title of Fuhrer, or "leader".

As leader, Hitler gradually and then with increasing rapidity began to impose his vision for a global German/Aryan ascendency. Domestically, he moved against those groups and peoples he and his adherents viewed as either sub-human, or direct threats to his authority. Internationally, he initiated a series of military expansions into neighboring counties.

The internal efforts to "cleanse" territory under German (and therefore Nazi) control escalated between 1939 and 1945 into what is now called the Holocaust: a systematic, professionalized, genocidal effort that killed more than ten million people (by conservative historical estimates), stripping Europe of its Jewish population. Two million Jewish children were among those slaughtered. The Nazis also targeted homosexual men and women, labor organizers, professors, artists, mentally and physically disabled people, Catholic priests, resistance fighters, Jehovah's Witnesses, Romanis, and many others.

The international seizure of territory triggered WWII, a conflict involving almost every country in the world. Soldiers and civilians suffered alike as the globe divided into the Nazi-aligned Axis, and the Allied counties. Battles were waged from the Sahara to the steppes of Russia; from the Pacific Islands to cold waters of the northern Atlantic. When combined with the casualties of Hitler's genocide, WWII and its fallout account for the deaths of more than sixty million people—at that time, nearly three percent of the world's population.

The savagery lasted until the war's end and beyond. After entering the war in late December 1941, the United States inexorably tipped the balance of battle in favor of the Allies, which began a slow march toward the site of the conflict's genesis: Berlin. But even as the German troops—spread thin, lacking supplies, and suffering from exhaustion, starvation, and exposure—retreated, Hitler's death-machine worked without pause, eliminating as many of the residents of concentration camps and prisons as possible.

Finally, as the Allies closed in from the west and the Russians from the east, Hitler took his own life. Eight days later, on May 8, 1945, Germany surrendered, ending the European conflict. On August, 6, America dropped an atomic bomb on Hiroshima, Japan, and a second bomb three days later on the city of Nagasaki. The Japanese surrendered on August 14, 1945. The war was over, but the toll it took on those who survived and the families of those who died continues to reverberate through the decades.

When confronted with devastation, the dead become a single, still image: a vast but two-dimensional mural of the macabre. If we view the Holocaust and WWII this way, we can be free of emotional detachment or horror.

But this is cowardice.

The magnitude of the Holocaust and WWII is not the breadth of the image but the brush strokes, each dipped in blood of a man, woman, child, a husband, a son, a wife, a poet, a dreamer, a dancer, a joker, a failure, a lover, a daughter, a coward, a mother, a holy man, a sister, a bully, a giver, a hero...no different than us.

The sound of war isn't the rattle of machine gun fire, or the bellowing of bombs. It is the voices of those who lived, and died. In this slender volume speak a few of those people who found themselves caught up in the horror of WWII in Europe—in the Holocaust, the battle zones of the Eastern and Western fronts, and in occupied

territories—and who call to us across time.
Open your heart and listen.

Elie Goldberg

How did it happen, tell me,
That I, the brightest in my field,
Dedicated to discovering truths,
Was one of the first to be deemed a threat?

And, how did it happen that I,
Who believed that knowledge alone
Could set us free,
Refused to see the encroaching infection?

As colleagues stood by, I was ripped from my classroom
And sent to a hell camp called Dachau,
Where labor, I was told, would set me free.
Arbeit Macht Frei...
Weak and weary, I died of smallpox that winter.

Now I, the brightest in my field,
Rest beneath the grass and ponder
The truths that lie outside of textbooks and beyond
reason.
Removed from pain, removed from gain, I *see*—

Not truth, nor work, but evil set me free...

Arbeit Macht Frei is German for the phrase "Work Will Set You Free." The saying was written above the front gates of several of Hitler's concentration camps, including Auschwitz, Dachau, Gross-Rosen and Terezin, in clear view of incoming inmates. It led them to believe that labor would be their salvation. Unfortunately, most were sent directly to the gas chambers.

Hitler realized that certain elements of society were in strong positions to speak out against Party ideals and to rally loyal followers. These included professors, teachers, clergy, and certain writers and artists. Accordingly, many of these professionals were removed under trumped-up charges and sent to concentration camps.

Ester Kaplan

I was seven when the soldiers came.
Mommy gave them *koch kaese*,
While I picked daisies for their collars,
And our lives began to end.

I was a laughing child with curly hair,
And flashing dark eyes.
I was strong and vibrant,
Well-fed by diet and affection.

With looks such as mine,
I needed no yellow star to label me Jewess.
The transports began.
My parents hid me in a Christian's basement.

They planted kisses on my cheeks and palms,
Promising to return, "soon."
Darkness became my daylight,
As I waited for "soon" to arrive.

Daily, I received bread and soup.
But my soul, starved of love,
Of touch, of lullabies, laughter,

And companionship began to die.

Then one day I soared
To a place where
Mothers sing and fathers tickle.
Where "soon"
Is never more than a hug away.

And I knew I was in heaven.

Koch kaese is a German pastry.

As the war progressed it was more and more difficult for families to leave occupied areas. Many countries refused to admit the immigrants and even when a welcoming host country was found, necessary papers and money for passage were unavailable. Parents were then forced to find hiding places for their families. In some instances it was necessary for children to be separated from their parents and secreted in orphanages, schools, farms, and churches. Some Jewish children were passed off as members of Christian families. Less fortunate children were housed in basements and attics, moved from location to location as necessary. If they survived the war, many of these hidden children returned to the outside world as orphans.

Rachel Stanz

They told me I was different—and I listened.
They told me to wear a star—so I stitched.
They told me to pack—so I gathered my things.
They told me to move—so I walked.

They told me to stay—so the ghetto became home.
They told me there was no food—so I starved.
They told me to leave—so I left.
They told me to flee—so I ran.

Bang...

They told me to die—so I slept.

Judah Birkowitz

Ba-ruch a-ta, A-do-nai E-lo-hei-nu

I was a man of G-d,
Who rose with the words of the morning prayer on my
lips.
"Mo-deh a-ni le-fa-ne-cha,"
And ended my days with thanks for Adonai's blessings.

I was a man of G-d,
Who believed we would be delivered from our tormentors.
I clung to faith in our Creator and in mankind
Long after smoke began to rise from the death camps.

I was a man of G-d,
Who knew of the pogroms, the Inquisition, and Diaspora
But couldn't believe, simply *couldn't believe*,
That we, the Chosen, would be called upon to suffer more.

I was a man of G-d,
Who lacked the strength to face the truth.
And so I told those who turned to me in confusion and
fear
To trust the very ones who led them to their deaths.

And now...

I am a man of G-d,
Who incants the Mourner's Kaddish throughout eternity.
And my soul cries out to a G-d I believed in,
A G-d who I failed, and a G-d who failed me.

Many Jews refuse to say or write the word "God" believing that the word itself is holy and should only be used in prayer. When referring to God outside of prayer, they might substitute the word, *Ha-shem*, meaning, "The name," (as in: Hashem created this beautiful day).

Hitler was a master propagandist who felt no compunction to tell the public the truth about his plans and actions unless doing so served him. He did his best to keep religious leaders ignorant of plans to kill them and their congregants in order to prevent outcry and rebellion. Nevertheless, some religious leaders *did* hear what was in store and were forced to decide what to do with the information.

Rivka Krylov

Sixteen, underdeveloped and painfully shy,
I was destined to die,
If not from the SS Einsatzgruppen's bullet,
Then from shame.

For there I stood,
At the pit's lip,
Stripped of shift, chemise, and stockings,
With Kliment Yosselevscka's eyes upon me.

And I knew that death couldn't come a moment too soon.

After German soldiers swept through occupied areas squads of
traveling killers would follow. These squads, the SS
Einsatzgruppen, marched victims to execution sites. There, the
doomed were ordered to undress because nude victims proved
to be less likely to protest or escape. The disrobing also made it
easier for the executioners to search victims' clothes for
valuables. The prisoners would be shot point-blank, their bodies
thrown into a previously-dug pit among the bodies of family and
neighbors. In some cases, steps were carved into the pit wall and
victims were forced at gunpoint to climb down into the hole and

lie upon the bodies of those who had been shot moments before. Once prone, they too would be murdered.

Kliment Yosselevscka

(Rivka Krylov's Classmate)

Stubborn to the end, my father refused to undress.
So they stripped him of his clothes,
And shot him.
He died angry.

My mother cradled a grandchild in her arms.
They stripped her of the infant,
Then shot them both.
She died wailing.

My little sister begged to be spared.
They stripped her of hope,
Teasing, taunting, then killing.
She died weeping.

But I left the world without complaint.
They could strip me of nothing but breath,
For across the dying,
Stood Ryvka, shimmering white and pure as prayer.

And I swore she would be my beacon to Paradise.

Victims of the SS Einsatzgruppen met their fates in many ways. Some were too shocked to protest. Some prayed. Some fought until they realized it was futile. A few attempted to escape and even fewer managed it—slipping away from the group as they were herded from their homes to the execution site. Others, survived their wounds and dragged themselves from the pit of corpses to hiding places after the killers had departed.

Sarah Anielewicz

I wore crimson ribbons in my hair,
A mile long, they climbed my braids
And fluttered, defiant as a knight's banner,
As I marched belligerently to the trains.

I wore crimson ribbons round my waist,
A half mile long, they cinched the prison
Sack that covered my unbent back,
As I stood furious, in lines.

I wore crimson ribbons in my boots,
A few feet long, they held the tattered
Leather scraps that covered festering feet,
As I marched defiantly to labors.

I wore crimson ribbons round my legs,
For days too long, they twined my calves,
Setting fire to my body and freeing my soul
To march glorified to God.

Labor and extermination camp prisoners suffered from
malnutrition, cold, exhaustion, and disease. Even minor injuries

could cause infections (the red ribbons that twined Sarah's legs) that spread due to lack of medical care. Even when medical help was available, prisoners were often turned away from camp clinics by physicians who claimed the inmates were simply being lazy. Many prisoners were reluctant to seek the camp doctor's assistance for fear they would be deemed unfit to work and therefore included on the next list for extermination. While death of prisoners was frequent, the tolls were especially high during epidemics of smallpox or epidemics of typhus, which was spread by fleas.

Jack Fajnzilber

They took us from the ghetto just as dawn broke,
My father, brother, little sister, and I,
And drove us like cattle to a sports field,
Where they began the sorting.
Right: strong. Left: old, young, and feeble.

We three were separated from little Tanya
By a thin rope that divided field and fates.
But as darkness lay its blanket
I stole heroically across the line to find my sister
And carry her, sobbing, toward life's side.

And then came the transports, the tattoos,
The camps, the labor, the beatings,
The rapes, the starvation, the corpses,
The horror, and terror, and agony,
The showers, the gas, and merciful Death.

And I, who watched my sister's suffering
From beyond a barrier of wood and wire,
Unable to touch or comfort her,
I wonder:
Did she die blessing or cursing me?

Males and females were usually separated in the death and labor camps (an exception were Gypsy prisoners who were often housed in family units) but could, upon occasion, make contact secretly through the barriers. Some survivors credit the bravery of those beyond the fences for keeping them alive by sharing procured food, clothing, and information.

Joshua Mahrer

My father was strong as Samson!
He could lift a wagon
Or even a house.
And he was smart too—really smart.
My father could kick a ball to the end of the earth.
He could fix anything.
When we went to the pond to fish
My father let me ride on his shoulders,
And we laughed and laughed.

My mother was pretty as a princess.
(Dad said so.)
She made the best *challah* in the village.
My mother was magic.
She could kiss scrapes better.
And when she sang,
Birds came to sit on the windowsill.
My mother wove blankets,
And fairytales, and good dreams.

When the Nazis came
My mother wrapped me in one of her blankets.
My father let them take us

To the woods by the pond where we fished.
And then they did nothing...
Nothing but hold me so I couldn't run.

I don't understand.

Challah is a braided bread used in a ceremony that greets the Jewish Sabbath on Friday evenings. After prayers, the bread is eaten as part of the Sabbath meal.

Those executed by Hitler's mobile killing squads often lived in small villages scattered throughout occupied areas. Off the beaten track, and out of touch with news of the day, these people had no way of knowing what horror awaited them. Had they known, had they believed, that they were to be murdered in cold blood, they might have fought back.

Louise Mahrer

(Joshua Mahrer's Mother)

...and God told Noah to build an arc.
Then they came aboard two by two.
As the water rose and rose.
And those aboard the boat were saved,
While those abandoned, forgotten,
Watched the rain pour, the waters rise,
Their homes flood,
Animals and fields drown.

And mothers looked into their children's eyes
And saw confusion turn to terror
As tiny hands clutched skirts
In pleading trust.
And, they could do nothing,
Nothing
But cling to each other,
And die.

And they call him A Loving God.

The story of Noah and the arc is found in Genesis, Chapters 6-8 of the Jewish holy book, the Torah (also called the Five Books of Moses).

Vera Zukoski

I was gifted
With ebony hair
And sapphire eyes.
My body was ripe and round,
Wrapped in milky skin
That made the soldiers groan
And grab and—moan.

I was gifted
With silver brushes and
Crimson flowers. Fruit
Juices dripped from my chin.
Milky chocolates plumped breasts
That heaved and swayed
As music danced—played.

I was gifted
With seductive magic
That turned the villagers envy green.
They tied my hair
To the tail of a horse
And drove it onward,
With jeers and laughter,

Here to sleep forever—after.

Insanity.
Vanity.

Some villagers in occupied areas welcomed, entertained, and assisted the Nazis, while giving up their Jewish neighbors and friends for deportation or execution.

Sonya Reichman

Terrified,
I shrank like a beaten pup
From the gaze of a cruel owner.
The soldier, suspicious of my cowering,
Accused me of a misdeed I hadn't committed.
Pointing his gun at my head, he laughed at my terror,
Then, in gentle voice, assuring me that my fear was
without cause,
He shot me once in each foot and the wounds infected.
My feet were amputated by a ghetto midwife.
So I could only listen to the uprising outside
As the brave ZOB ghetto fighters resisted
More death deportations to Treblinka.
Then there was defeat and silence.
Buildings were set to flame.
And I was unable to
Run.

Some Jews were forced to live in ghettos during the war. These
walled, or fenced-off, neighborhoods were located in poorer
sections of cities. Ghetto conditions were abominable.
Starvation, disease, and cold killed many. In 1940, the Nazis

moved four hundred thousand Jews into an area two-and-a-half miles long and a mile wide. By 1942, only about sixty thousand Jews remained in the Warsaw Ghetto, the others having died, or been shipped to camps. Upon hearing of plans to ship remaining ghetto residents to the death camp of Treblinka, Jewish leaders organized a resistance. With smuggled and homemade weapons, they fired upon the Nazis from rooftops and sewer holes. The uprising lasted a month. A reported fifty-six thousand Jews were either killed, captured or burned when the Nazis set the area on fire. Although reports on Nazi causalities vary, some say three hundred soldiers were killed and another one thousand injured in the uprising.

The ZOB (Zydowska Organizacja Bojowa) was a Jewish Fighting Organization that encouraged those living in the ghetto to resist deportment.

Noah Kotmel

The diamonds shone like broken glass,
Recklessly dumped from wooden trays.
They twinkled on the floor
For a heartbeat,
Before scattering under stomping boots.

The broken glass shone like teardrops,
Exploding in angry shouts.
Razor shards ripped flowered paper from walls
For a heartbeat,
Before scattering under stomping boots.

The teardrops shone like diamonds,
Flowing in torrents from Jewish eyes.
Women screamed, men moaned, synagogues burned
For a heartbeat,
Before our true horror began.

November 10, 1938, the Nazis organized a night of mayhem in response to the killing of a German diplomat by a Jewish teen. During the night and early morning hours, Germans were told to show their fury by destroying Jewish property. Mobs of

Germans broke the glass windows and doors of approximately seven thousand five hundred Jewish shops. One hundred and ninety-one synagogues were destroyed, as well as many homes. Some Jewish women were raped and more than ninety Jews were killed. This incident, in which streets were strewn with broken glass, became known as *Kristallnacht*, or Crystal Night.

Odo Wilhelm
(Nazi Soldier)

They tell of the suffering of Untermenschen
With quivering lips, indignation, fury.
They clutch breasts and shake heads,
While speaking of "monsters in our midst."
But do they tell of the German people's suffering;
The starvation, loss of jobs, and land?
Do they tell how dishonest Jews
Caused that plague of misery and death
That descended on our country after the first war?
Is it no wonder that, as a beaten dog,
Driven mad with hunger and pain,
Will turn on its tormentor,
We turned on the Jews?

They tell of the suffering of Untermenschen
With quivering lips, indignation, and fury.
They make me sick.

Untermenschen or "sub-humans" was Hitler's term for non-Aryans. These included Jews, Slavs, southern Europeans, and all non-white people. Hitler and his followers believed that Untermenschen were fit only to serve Aryan Germans while consuming as little resources and space as possible.

Germany was a country in crises after WWI. The Treaty of Versailles, signed in June 1919, forced Germany to give up a seventh of its land and all of its overseas holdings. It also required Germany to pay large financial settlements to the war's victors. Many Germans starved in the years following the war because damaged transportation systems made it impossible to get food to the hungry. There was a shortage of jobs, and German money was valueless. Germans sought to place the blame for their suffering. Some pointed fingers at the government, some at the banks, some at manufacturers, and others at the unions. But, in a country with a long-established history of anti-Semitism, the most popular scapegoat was the Jews.

Grietje Kuilema

I was the child of money and position,
Who wished and wanted for nothing,
Except that *glorious* Thais Staalekker.

Dashing, daring, and brilliant,
Filled with ideal and driven by honor,
Thais worked with the Dutch Resistance.

And I, determined to snare the prize,
Became involved in exhausting intrigue,
Smuggling ration coupons to Jew-Hiders.

Upon discovering Thais loved Lilly Rienks,
I publicly denounced him as a traitor,
And smiled upon hearing the gunshot.

Hell hath no fury like a woman scorned.

Most occupied countries had groups of resistance fighters who
routinely sabotaged factories and transports, rescued Allied
soldiers, supplied arms and information to ghetto populations,
hid those who were being hunted, engaged in guerilla warfare

against Nazi troops, kept underground railroads operative, and did what they could in other ways to disable Nazi efforts. In order to deter these groups, Nazi leaders ordered retaliatory actions. Each time a German soldier or civilian was killed by a resistance fighter, a certain number of randomly-selected hostages would be shot. Sometimes the ratio would be one hundred retaliatory executions for a single killing by a resistance soldier.

Lilly Rienks

(Thais Staalekker's Lover)

As a moth is drawn to flame,
Man is drawn to a passionate woman.
As a moth is drawn to flame,
Such a woman is drawn to a superior man.
Minds and bodies linked, moving as one,
They explode into a firestorm of blue heat—
Capable of redirecting the Earth's rotation.

When such a God-directed phenomena is doused
By tear-soaked acts of a jealous shrew,
The world tilts on its axis.
As a moth is drawn to flame,
A grieving woman is drawn to revenge.
The embers of my smoldering heart and a kitchen match
Sent Grietje Kuileme home into Satan's arms.

I followed, in my own good time.

Sonya Griendling

I lifted spirits and hearts,
With a body flexible as taffy,
Stretched taut and strong.
As gazelles leap,
Butterflies dip and sway,
As hummingbirds' wings spin,
I was born to dance.

Raised at a ballet barre;
Cabrioles and devéoppés'
Carved legs that defied gravity.
Chest lifted, arms rounded,
Muscles groaning, shrieking,
Heartbeat throbbing,
I soared to thundering applause.

From revered heights
To catastrophic low,
I was herded into a stock car
That chugged toward a misery
I was unprepared to face,
In a base labor camp
Bereft of music, of beauty.

Artists, Communists, Jews,
Gypsies were packed together.
Desperate, they ripped away
The wagon window's wire cage,
And I, chest lifted, arms rounded,
Heartbeat throbbing,
Leapt one last time.

Prisoners bound for labor and death camps were transported in cattle cars. Tightly-packed, there was no room for prisoners to sit or lie down, and some died of suffocation. The cars were unheated in the winter and uncooled in the summer. They lacked bathroom facilities. Victims were forced to travel three to four days without food or drink. Many, especially those already weak or ill, died before reaching their destination. Desperate, some prisoners pulled the planks from the car's floor and attempted to escape by lowering themselves between the wheels of the train. Others pulled the wire mesh from the ventilation windows and jumped from the moving car. If the fall didn't kill them, they were often shot by soldiers stationed on top of the train.

Kurt Smolitz

You! Yes! You, passing by,
Hear my words.
I was one of fifty healthy boys
Chosen to be lab rats
In that ambitious doctor's
Decompression experiments.

But my father, hearing whispers
Of unfathomable agonies
And unkind deaths,
Secreted me under his cot.
So the guards filled their quota
With another healthy boy.

I died of guilt and shame
That my good fortune
Sent another child into the night,
With bursting eardrums,
Eyes leaping from sockets,
And pained madness.

If you see that boy in your wanderings,
Tell him I'm sorry.

Sigmund Rascher, a German doctor, used prison inmates in a number of grisly medical experiments. He was particularly interested in the effects of high altitudes on pilots, and ran tests in which victims were placed in a decompression chamber. The young, healthy prisoners were then subjected to extremely high pressures, resulting in agonizing deaths. Rascher was not alone in conducting morbid medical experiments. Other physicians systematically infected prisoners with typhus and froze, dissected, and maimed them as well as surgically and pharmaceutically sterilizing men and women. Dr. Fritz Ernst Fischer attempted to transplant bones of living victims.

Victoria Czastkiewicz

...and it had a pink ribbon here,
And another one here,
On the shoulder!
And the ruffle went from right here,
To 'round over here.
Two layers!
And the petticoats made it stick out—
Like a tent—like this.
Mama made the lace herself
And sewed it in waves
All 'round the collar.
It was my specialist dress,
My *Shabbat* dress.
When they came for us,
Mama put me in it,
(though it was only Thursday).
Everyone was crying
When those soldiers lifted
Their guns, but I wasn't
Even a littlest bit scared
Because I *knew* even bad Nazis
Would never, *ever*
Ruin such a pretty dress
With bullet holes.

Shabbat, the Jewish Sabbath, begins at sundown on Friday evening and ends at sundown the next day. It is celebrated by the lighting of candles, prayer, study, and a special meal.

Two million Jewish children were murdered during the Holocaust, making up a quarter of the six million Jews who lost their lives. Many were shot, some were burned or buried alive, and others were killed in concentration and death camps.

Klaus Sichrovsky
(German Soldier)

A member of the German Young Folk: age ten.
A member of the Hitler Youth: age fifteen.
A child spy in the Streifendienst: age sixteen.
Fathered a pure Aryan son: age seventeen.
Married a pure Aryan wife: age eighteen.
Joined the SS Einsatzgruppen: age nineteen.
Executed Untermenschen at Zagrodski: age twenty.
Died in the Battle of Berlin: age twenty-five.

So few years. So much accomplished!

The SS Einsatzgruppen were killing squads assigned the task of rounding up and killing Jewish men, but eventually they included women and children in their mass murders. Victims were often shot point-blank, though sometimes they were gassed in mobile killing vans that pumped carbon monoxide into compartments that held between eighty and one hundred fifty victims.

The Battle of Berlin was fought between German and Allied forces in April 1945. Large numbers of Hitler Youth fought in the battle. More than four thousand were reportedly killed.

"*Untermenschen*" or "sub-humans," was a term used by Hitler to describe those he considered inferior, including Jews, Gypsies, non-Aryans, Slavs, Southern Europeans, and all non-white races. German youth were raised to believe in Hitler's bigoted position and to do what was necessary to insure the domination of the Pure Aryan Race.

Niklas Renke

(German Soldier)

She had the tongue of an asp
That stung an agonizing wound,
And the face of a sewer rat
With teeth rabidly ready
To inflict writhing convulsions.
She drove my father's lips to the bottle
And his body to the village whore.
In me, she planted such a putrid seed
Of hate for the stench of female
That I turned, forever, the other way.
How ironic, then, that I should die,
Face-to-face with a *chaluzim* she-devil,
Who licked taunting, slug lips
That curved in a feline grin.
Captured, but not resigned,
She pulled the pin on a grenade
Secreted beneath her clothes.
And, together, we met our fate.

Chaluzim, Jewish women guerrilla fighters, were considered especially ferocious. There are reports in which they met their opponents, firing pistols with both hands. Rather than allowing themselves to be captured and taken prisoner, they would pull the pins on hand grenades concealed in their underwear. In this way, they were assured that their captors would die with them. The Nazis, who strongly believed that women should keep house and bear children, considered these *chaluzim* to be especially disconcerting.

Johanna Stine
(Chalutz)

Hatshepsut—15th Century B.C., Queen of Egypt
Nefertiti—14th Century B.C., Queen of Egypt
Sammuramat—9th Century B.C., Assyrian Queen
Cleopatra—69-30 B.C., Queen of Egypt
Elenor of Aquintaine—1122-1202, Queen of England and
France
Joan of Arc—1412-31, Leader of the French Army
Isabella I of Castile—1451-1504, Queen of Spain
Catherine de Medici—1519-1589, Queen of France
Mary Queen of Scots—1542-1587
Elizabeth I—1533-1603
Amina—1560-1610, Nigerian Queen
Mbande Nzinga—1582-1663, Angolan Queen
Catherine the Great—1729-96, Empress of Russia
Victoria—1818-1901, Queen of England
Tzu-his—1835-1908, Empress of China
Liliuokalani—1838-1917, Last Monarch of Hawaii...
Johanna Stine—1922-1942, Chalutz

The weaker sex?
Hah!

Chaluzim were fearless Jewish female warriors who, when captured, would often take their own lives. In ghetto uprisings they would fire from rooftops and pop up out of sewer holes to shoot enemy soldiers.

Gerbert Ludwig

(Member of Hitler Youth Group)

"Live faithfully,
Fight bravely,
And die laughing."
No fairytales nor childish rhymes for me!
I teethed on the motto of the Hitler Youth.
Puberty brought torturous lust
To give body and soul
To the great and noble cause.
I breathed the party line.
Heil Hitler!

Streifendienst!
How honored to be
A Nazi child spy!
I turned in the grocer across the street
Who blamed the Nazis, not the rabble,
For shortages of bread and meat.
I turned in the village priest

For teaching that all men are equal
In the eyes of God.
Heil Hitler!

When my father,
A weak, disgusting man,
Talked about hiding
A Jewish family in our basement
I cut the cancer from our midst
And turned him in as well.
Later, I fell in battle and was left where I lay.
Still, no taste of regret lingered on my lips...
Though my mother's curses still rang in my ears.
Heil Hitler!

Streifendienst was a sub-group of the Hitler Youth. Formed in 1938, children selected for inclusion in this elite group were responsible for monitoring the conversations and activities of those within their communities, and reporting those potentially harboring anti-Nazi sentiments to officials.

The Hitler Youth was first organized in 1922. By 1926, it was an official part of the Nazi party. The group was divided into two sections: the German Young Folk for boys ages ten through fourteen, and the Hitler Youth for boys ages fifteen through eighteen.

Herta Kaufmann

(Member of Hitler Youth Group)

From the body of this child
Another child strained to emerge,
But I, only twelve, couldn't—
I tried, but, Oh God,
I just *couldn't* allow him passage.
Blood flowed from my womb
To stain snowy sheets.
I mewed and wailed,
Crying out, "Mama, help!"
She could do nothing
But stroke my brow
And croon a soothing lullaby
As I left the world,
Taking my baby soldier with me.
In this, I failed my Fuehrer.

German girls became part of the Hitler Youth in 1927. Their motto, "Be Faithful, Be Pure, Be German!" was embraced by members who were told that their moral and patriotic responsibility was to bear children for Hitler's Reich. If possible, this should be accomplished within wedlock, but there was no shame in out-of-wedlock pregnancy. Many young girls became pregnant in zealous attempts to fulfill their patriotic duty.

Jan Kowolski

What would you do if you were only eighteen
and put in a ghetto where your mother and sister starved,
then sent with your father to a labor camp
to rise before dawn, discovering your bedmates dead,
then roll call—four hours in driving snow or soul searing
heat—
and you couldn't wear your hat so it beat on your head,
while the man beside you buckled and collapsed and
another
was dealt a rib-crushing blow and another muttered
insanities
and another, covered in pustules and burning with fever,
vomited on your shoes and another was shot before your
eyes
and then hours walk to a job hauling heavy bags of
concrete
until your back bent and holes in your feet bled and oozed
and breakfast was a piece of bread and lunch, thin soup,
and the yells and the screams and the slams and
babies tossed into the air for target practice
and you can see your bones through your skin
and children unloaded from trains, gas,
and mothers screaming, children crying

and your tooth aches
and smoke and smells
and you just can't bear it,
you just can't bear it
you just can't bear it
what would you do?

I wasn't trying to escape.
Just to die.

Eva Wilenski

Once upon a time

There was a fat ratt named Lech.
He bit off Gittel's tale.
(She wouldn't let him snuggle.)
Sometimes, they let me pet them.
(When they wanted my bred.)
Papa said, "Dont share!
There's not enuf for us,"
(Let alone the rats!)
The sanitashun workers droped food
Through the sewer holes.
And we waited in the cold
For the war to end.
I played with the ratts
And tried to keep my feet dry.
And sometimes I wondered
What the ghetto looked like now.
I tried to remember
How the sun felt on the bak of my neck,
And how flowers smeled,
And what wind wispers in your ear.
Mama's baby was born.

(It went to heaven.)
One day Lech bit me.
And I went to join the baby
And God.

The end.

When those living in the Lvov Ghetto in Poland heard of Nazi plans to liquidate the area, some moved into the sewers. There they lived for more than a year in the bitter, cold, rat-infested damp. They couldn't talk above a whisper for fear of being heard by those above ground. Sympathetic sanitation workers provided the hiders with food and supplies. Some of the hunted died of cold or disease. Others couldn't handle the conditions and surrendered. When Allied troops liberated Lvov, the younger children, who had spent a good part of their lives underground, were terrified of daylight and city noise.

Baby Wilenski

(Eva Wilenski's Baby Brother)

Bathed in glowing light.
Through a tunnel dark and deep.
A triumphant victory cry.
"I have arrived!"
The most beautiful face in the world.
A butterfly kiss.
A croon.
"Hush, love, hush."
A bosom soft and sweet.
"*Shut it up!*"
"*Make it stop!*"
"*Someone will hear!*"
Weathered hands on fragile skin.
Then—
Back into the angels' arms.

Hidden in sewers, behind walls, in basements, and attics, silence was imperative for survival. It was hard enough to keep young children quiet day after day, week after week, year after year. But it was virtually impossible to keep infants from crying. Their wailing jeopardized the lives of those secreted away and so, in some cases, they were sacrificed for the safety of the others.

Astana Kovalov

In those cruel nights when God was not,
In those cruel nights and endless days
That crept by in a bleary haze
Of groans and whimpers, muffled low,
Like fearful footsteps in the snow,
I thought, if I am ever whole
There will be nothing in my soul
That has survived this agony—
And then one night I woke to see
A comet streaking through the night.
It quickly slipped out of my sight—
Yet in that moment I forgot
The wretched days when God was not.

The thoughts, feelings, and experiences of a small number of prisoners of labor and death camps as well as those forced into hiding were written down. An even smaller number of these accounts made it through the war, such as *The Diary of Anne Frank*—an account of a young girl's years in hiding in the annex of a building in Amsterdam, Holland. War victims who hadn't access to diaries wrote their stories on pieces of toilet paper, small pieces of scrap paper, walls and even fabric. Writing tools such as pencils could be bartered in exchange for personal possessions within the camps.

Sonja Rosenberg

Tragedy is to be born with a poet's soul
Into a life of peasant's poverty.
I dreamed of having time to dream,
To pen words that would make my family proud.
But there was laundry to do,
Bread to bake,
Children to wash, and scold, and hug,
A husband to love and listen to,
A house to clean,
Prayers to say,
The elderly to visit,
Friends to nurture,
The sick to tend,
The garden to weed and water,
Food to put up,
Clothes to press,
Shopping,
Animals to feed and groom,
Steps to sweep, and sweep, and sweep again.
Courage to summon,
And bullets to take.
Now I lie here spinning verse after verse.
And nobody is left to read them.

Kerry Arquette

Resi Hoffmeir

What if you knew that your child died in a gas chamber?
What if you knew that your child was executed?
What if you knew that your child was starved?
What if you knew that your child suffocated in a transport?
What if you knew your child was experimented upon?
What if you knew your child froze to death?
What if you knew your child had been given a poison
injection?

Could it possibly be as bad, I ask you,
As never knowing what happened to your child—
And spending eternity weeping and wondering and
worrying
That he died frightened and alone?

Those transported to labor and death camps were given little
notice or time for preparation. Often roused in the middle of the
night by a pounding at their door and the yelling of soldiers'
voices, they were allowed to pack a few personal items before
being ordered or driven to the nearest train stop. In the frenzied
crowd of terrified humans, and the hurried loading of cattle cars,
children were sometimes separated from their parents. Train

trips lasted days to weeks. When the cars were unloaded at the other end, reunions were uncertain.

Elizabeth Stern

What a terrible decision,
A seemingly impossible decision!
But the boy's sobs
Tore me from my daughter's side.
I scooped up the lost toddler,
Soothing him with gentle whispers.
And when the sorting came,
My daughter, almost a woman,
Was chosen to live on
While those with small children were sent
Toward the gas chambers.
"Is that your baby?" the soldier demanded.
I looked over the tiny head,
Resting heavily on my shoulder,
Into my lovely daughter's eyes.
And we said goodbye.
For how could I allow a child to
Walk into death's arms terrified and alone?
There was no decision to be made,
No decision at all.

After being transported to the death camps and unloaded from the trains, prisoners were herded into lines for the sorting process. The procedure was brutal, with soldiers beating the prisoners at random while screaming directions in languages the deportees couldn't understand. In the mayhem children were sometimes separated from their parents. At the sorting a Nazi officer separated young, fit men and women capable of working from those who would be immediately exterminated—the young, old, or ill. Mothers with young children were automatically sent to the gas chambers.

Unknown

No one noticed the shadow child
Who hid beneath the stairs to read,
And watched the shining, gifted ones
Exchange their birthday party talk,
Or chat about the games they played
At get-togethers after school.

While her heart cried out,
I'm here! I'm here!

No one noticed the mousy teen
Who viewed the world from downcast eyes.
She longed for boys with cocky grins,
And envied girls with flowing hair.
She ached to join their weekend plans
And laughing talk of who-likes-who.

While her heart cried out,
I'm here! I'm here!

No one noticed the silent woman
Who slid through days so calm and still
That when the Nazis plucked her up

And worked her hard, then put her down,
The world went on without a hitch.
And no one said, "Where did She go?"

Still her heart cries out,
I'm here! *I'm here*!

As extermination, fighting, and other threats depleted the German work force, the Nazis looked to occupied countries to replenish their dwindling labor force. When citizens of German occupied areas refused to volunteer for deportation and work, they were recruited against their will. Eastern workers, or *Ostarbeiter*, were ruthlessly snatched from public areas such as stores, cinemas, churches, and parks. Their disappearance was not explained to frantic family members and friends left behind. Terrible work conditions for these slave laborers killed off many and they were buried anonymously in foreign soil.

Andre Petit

One heartbeat in
One child's chest in
One family's home in
One tiny town in
One part of France in
One awful war

Was stilled

by

One measure of gas in
One monster's hand in
One hellish place in
One evil moment in
One blast of hatred in
One heartbeat.

The Germans entered Paris, France in June 1940. Under an agreement between the French and Germans, France was divided into two zones. The northern half of the country was occupied and controlled by the Germans. The southern part of

France, known as Vichy, was to remain unoccupied and under French control. Almost immediately after the establishment of the Vichy regime, the occupied French leadership began establishing their own anti-Semitic policies. Independently, and in cooperation with the Germans, the French participated in roundups and deportations of Jews to Hitler's death camps. Between seventy thousand and eighty thousand French Jews were killed during the Holocaust.

Justified

Odilo was a bad man, well-suited for his job.
With glowing red eyes and a feral grin,
He panted his way toward climactic bellows
As the young mother's head splattered
Like an egg on paving stones.
Spittle dripped from his smiling lips,
To the naked breasts of the sprawled body.
He holstered his gun and laughed.

I was a good man, who hated his job.
My eyes teared at the mother's terror,
And flowed at the sight of her orphaned child.
Blood-and-brain-splattered, shivering,
He watched, stunned, as I raised my gun.
For without his mother, the child was alone,
To wander and starve and freeze.
A good man would never let a child suffer.

The Einsatzkommando 3, mobile killing units, were often made
up of two-man teams. When executions were done at close
quarters, they would select two victims to be simultaneously
executed. The face-to-face murders were believed to take an

emotional toll on many of the killers, who dulled themselves with alcohol. The Nazis viewed the use of poison gas as less traumatic on their executioners, as well as more efficient and less time-consuming.

Marina Tereshkova

A lovely little life in a little lovely house awaited me.
There, warmed by hearth fire,
Slow molasses days would pass
As simple verses flowed from my pen,
And cloying proverbs in pastel thread, from my needle.

In that cottage, quaint and calm,
My love would find me waiting at day's end,
With cheek at ready so his lips might press home the
obligatory kiss.
Then into eve and on through dinner
Trifling talk of this and that would fill the silence until bed
beckoned.

Resting by his side, serenaded by rolling snores,
I would contemplate a woman's fate;
How nicely-ordered, how profitably full
Of church bazaars, book chats, coffee klatches, gentle
gossip,
Adoring children and grateful, dimming parents.

A lovely little life in a lovely house awaited me.
There, hips spreading, breasts sagging, mind bored-
numbed,
Hair tucked up, eyes modestly downcast,
I might have passed long, languishing years
Contently grounded in mundanity.

But a woman whose heart beats a machine gun cadence
At talk of politics, intrigue or battle,
Was not created for hearth and home.
Born with a banshee's scream in my throat,
I never questioned my destiny:
For how much finer to die young, in a blaze of glory for
Mother Russia
Than to live and live and live, and never live at all!

In 1942, Russia began using women as combat pilots. They flew
both bomber and fighter planes on missions that often took
place after nightfall. Feared by the Germans for their aggression,
skill, and daring, they were called Night Witches.

Lola Krantz

The table was covered in shimmery white linen,
And tall candles stood proudly in silver holders.
Matzah, bitter herbs, eggs, haroset, maror—
The Feast of Passover spread before us
As we listened to Papa read from the *Haggadah*.
In the flickering flames, the ancient story took shape,
With Moses beseeching Pharaoh to let his people go.
The plagues descended like a pall over Egypt,
And my heart ached for those who suffered.
With toasts of Sanctification, Redemption, and
Deliverance,
We marked our ancestors' escape from servitude,
Their wanderings, and arrival in the Promised Land.
Just as Papa raised the final cup—the glass of
Acceptance—
The door to our house flung open and in They poured,
Tipping the lovely table on its side,
Sending candles and plates crashing to the floor.
Papa, Mama, and I were dragged to the yard
And lined against the white washed wall.
As the soldiers lifted their guns I heard Papa's voice
defiantly
Proclaiming the last words of our Seder service,

"Next year, may we all be in Jerusalem!"
And I started to cry for I realized
I would soon be dead and so...
Would never live to see that cherished dream fulfilled.

Jews celebrate the week-long holiday of Passover with a Seder service held within the home. The service is printed in a special prayer book, a Haggadah, that contains prayers and may include songs. It recounts the story of the Jews escape from servitude and their exodus from Egypt with Moses. The Seder service involves the eating of special foods. The conclusion of each service calls Jews back to their homeland.

Adele Opfer

Once I saw a perfect rose
Of untold luscious, peachy hue,
Its petals, velvet teardrops, spread
Seductively to catch the dew.

I wanted to possess the bloom
But knew that it could not be mine.
To punish both the rose and me,
I tore the flower from the vine.

Once I was that perfect rose
Who caught a German unaware.
He knew that I had Jewish blood,
But lusted for my golden hair.

He wanted to possess the bloom,
And, angered that it couldn't be,
He ordered that I should be killed.
So, dust to dust—the rose and me.

It is said that Dr. Josef Mengele, Auschwitz's "Angel of Death,"
would become infatuated with beautiful female prisoners. In

questioning them, he would ask personal questions that seemed to titillate his imagination. Reports tell of one particularly beautiful Jewish teen who captured the attentions of Mengele. Seemingly infuriated by his response to the girl, he used her for his experiments on female reproductive organs. When seen several weeks later by other prisoners, the girl was bloated, dazed, and almost unrecognizable. She died soon thereafter.

Lidia Klimenko

I was young and terrified
When taken from my Motherland,
For I had heard the nightmare tales
Of horrors that awaited me.
But luck's eye fell upon my face,
And I became a Captain's maid.
Oh, he was dashing, kind, and strong,
And generous in sharing love.

Sometimes in my Captain's bed
I prayed the war would never end.
My heart was full. I closed my mind
To sufferings outside his arms.
Then came the day we heard the news
That I must travel home—alone,
Where hissing cries of "Nazi whore,"
And certain death awaited me.

Each step along the grisly path,
The dusty, corpse-lined, trodden road
I scattered pieces of my heart,
For empty-breasted scavengers
To pluck and sort and piece and glue.

I envied them the faith to hope
A fractured heart might beat again.
But things so shattered never mend.
And why live on bereft of love?

After World War II ended Russians who had been arrested and used as slave laborers were required to return to their native country. Those who went back were often viewed as traitors and killed by their countrymen. Suicide, it was believed, was a preferred choice for many captured patriotic Russians.

Leoind Gerbrandt
(German Soldier)

There is a cold that
Sears a man's soul,
A flame blue cold
That turns tears to sabers
And cauterizes eyelids closed.

There is a cold that
Knocks oxen off frozen feet
And makes horses glisten like marble.
In its grip, tree limbs
Splinter like ancient bones.

There is a cold that
Makes crystal sand of breath.
It sneaks through buttonholes
And writhes in and out of thread tracks
To gnaw fingertips to knuckles.

There is a cold that
Adheres damp tongues

Kerry Arquette

To the roofs of mouths
So a dying man's last mewing word,
"Mama!"
Sounds much like his first.

The winter of 1941 was especially brutal in Russia with wind-whipped days dropping to minus forty degrees Fahrenheit. When invading German soldiers died of frostbite and shock, the frozen ground made burial impossible. For additional warmth, the soldiers wrapped themselves in stolen tablecloths and sheets. Legs were sawed from dead soldiers and heated in ovens so the boots could be removed to be used by other men. Fluids in trains, cars, even guns, froze. Nearly one hundred thousand German military horses died and were eaten.

Golly Sussman

Mine was a quiet world, a peaceful world and rich.
There, cinnamon tasted like sugared fire on a tongue
And milk wasn't gulped, it slid down a throat like white
satin.
I could greet a flower by name long before I saw its face
For flowers, like garden herbs, are as distinct as French
perfume.
I worked with a needle that was sharp and quick as my
mind,
Creating tapestries that told the stories of God's miracles.
In the afternoon, when the wind called through the
window, I left my work
And danced on the sun-dappled lawn to mind music.
And, in my fiancée's eyes, I saw all the love songs ever
sung.

My love and I dreamed of a child with whom to share this
world.
But the Nazis could no more celebrate our dreams
Than could they see my worth or taste my joy in life.
Unable to feel the thrill of God in their own hearts,
They denied His existence and snatched His power

To decide who would conceive and bear children.
Claiming my "deaf genes" would taint the German pool,
They ordered their surgeon to seal my womb.
The cries of my unborn child now drown out any whispers
of pity
I might feel for men as handicapped as these.

In 1933, the Nazis put into effect the Law for the Prevention of Progeny with Hereditary Diseases, which mandated the sterilization of those with certain disabilities including some mental illnesses, "retardation," physical deformities, epilepsy, blindness, and deafness. (The Nazis burned books written by Helen Keller, who overcame her deafness to become a respected writer and a symbol of strength of the human spirit.) Over the following years, more than three hundred thousand people are believed to have been sterilized.

The Never-To-Be Born

...

Seymour Poppanick

Physician, you put your bloodied hands around the neck of
a babe
And yanked me, impatiently, recklessly, from my mother's
body,
Tightening the sinewy cord wrapped around my neck
Like a constrictor's squeeze that starved my fluttering brain
of oxygen.
In those moments of tug and tangle you turned me from
miracle to monster.

Physician, slumped and bound in a chair or prone and
ignored in a crib,
I jerked, slobbered, and moaned away twenty years.
All the while, through mist-shrouded reality, pressed vague
images
Of all that I would never, *could* never, experience...
Love, home, purpose, joy, strength, desire, passion, hope.

Physician, you then put your bloodied hands around the
arm of a man
And slid a slender needle deep into my throbbing vein.
As the poison flowed, the fog lifted and I rejoiced in the
truth,

That I will meet God pure of heart and soul while *you*,
doctor,
Will be judged for stealing my life—twice.

In 1939, Hitler ordered the initiation of a "euthanasia program," which specified the killing of mentally and physically handicapped people. While Hitler called these executions "mercy deaths," their real purpose was to cleanse the German population of "defective" genes. Victims were bussed to killing centers where they were killed by lethal injection. Later, gas was deemed a more efficient method of extermination. The "euthanasia program," code named Operation T4, was conducted in secret because of feared public opposition. However, word got out, and by 1941, public pressure forced the project to shut down publically, although the executions continued throughout the war. The number of victims murdered in the program is unknown, however experts estimate that between 1940 and 1945 more than two hundred thousand were killed.

Johann Goldschmitt

A priest is nothing without faith.
That is what links him to God, whom he serves.
It inspires questions, provides answers,
And is the seed, water, and sun for courage.
In Dachau, our beliefs were our identifying collar.
I, newly ordained, shone with knowledge of His glory
And ached for opportunities to prove my
Faith.

A priest is nothing without conviction.
I tried to cling to my beliefs with terrified passion.
But exhausted, ill men are spiritually vulnerable,
And doubt feasts on vulnerability like infection on open
flesh.
I filled my head and heart with droning prayer
To drown out the condemning screams of souls
Who watched and bemoaned my failing
Faith.

A priest is nothing without religious fervor.
I prayed for a chance to reclaim my own.
Then came the day the Tormentors decided
Ten prisoners would be killed for one who escaped.

A doomed man wept in terror until a priest stepped into
his place.
And that holy martyr met God wrapped in glory.
While I, a *nothing* priest, mourned my dead
Faith.

The concentration camp at Dachau housed an estimated 2,579
Catholic priests and other clergymen. These "special prisoners"
were kept largely isolated from the rest of the inmates. While
their living conditions were no better than the prison populous
at large, some priests were allowed to celebrate Mass, hear
confession, give absolution, and tend to the sick and dying. In
July 1941, Father Maximilian Kolbe, voluntarily took the place of
a condemned prisoner—a man with a wife and child. Father
Kolbe joined nine other men in a "hunger-bunker" where all
starved for two weeks after which those men still living were
killed by lethal injection. He died on August 14, 1941.

Renee Robota

"Through remorse, confession and penitence we are
saved."
That's what the Fathers said.

But I didn't feel remorse
When I stole the cookies from the jar
And Baby Peter got blamed,
Or when I called Marta a name so bad
Even I was shocked-red
When it came popping out of my mouth.

I didn't confess
When I broke Bubbie's vase.
(I swore the dog's tail did it.)
And no way was I going to tell
When I put my peas in my napkin
And the napkin in my shoe in the closet.

I did no penitence
When I ripped my special-dress hem.
I stuck it back on with schoolroom glue
(And tutted when it came apart in the wash)
Or when I hid in the tree all afternoon
And scared Papa half to death.

Nobody knew how bad I was except
God
Who let me go to my death
Babbling about my sins and
Sobbing
"I'm sorry! I'm sorry! I'm sorry!"

Werner Mueller

(German WWI Veteran)

I offered to fight but they laughed me away,
"Old man, go tend your sheep."
Bowed, gray, and humiliated,
I wrapped tatters of my self-esteem
In remnant memories of another war,
In another lifetime when I
Was the same man in a younger body.
And I did heroic things.

Then they handed me arms,
So I left my flock to a legless soldier,
And set out to fight Germany's war.
Each creaking, painful step forward, took me back,
Toward a time when I had purpose and pride.
An old heart beat a young man's cadence
Once again in my shallow chest.
And I did heroic things.

I fell, a defeated Nazi soldier.
I fell, a victorious, vibrant Man.

As the war neared its end and Russian troops advanced into Germany, members of the German *Volkssturm*, or the Home Guard, were called upon to take up arms. These troops consisted of men under the age of sixteen and as old as seventy. Russian journalists voraciously snapped photos of older Nazi soldiers and distributed them as part of a morale-boosting propaganda campaign. A far cry from Hitler's "idealized Aryan God-like Nazi males," these soldiers were grizzled and stooped.

Hans Feldman

(German Soldier)

... like sheep to the slaughter.

They watched their possessions being confiscated.
They allowed their homes to be taken away.
They docilely gave up their jobs and professions.
They did nothing when their children were barred from school.
They relocated with little protest.
They moved into hellholes of ghettos and overcrowded tenements.
They sewed identifying stars on their clothes, when instructed.
They ceased to congregate for religious worship.
They followed edicts disallowing them access to parks and public places.
They let their cities be overrun and ruled by strangers.
They resigned themselves to beatings and other humiliations.
They watched their neighbors massacred.
They dug pits, stepped in, and waited for the bullets.

They complied when told to meet for deportation.
They permitted their families to be separated.
They boarded the trains.
They walked to the gas chambers.
They worked until they dropped, making war goods for
their enemy.

And they never lifted a finger to save themselves!

Nazis began to move against Jews as early as April 1933, when they staged a boycott of Jewish shops and businesses. That same year they excluded Jews from the arts and prohibited them from owning land. Further anti-Semitic acts followed. In 1934 Jews were disallowed national health insurance. The following year Jews were banned from serving in the military. In 1937, they were banned from many other professions. In 1938, further restrictions were put on Jewish businessmen, and Jewish doctors and lawyers were no longer allowed to practice. That same year Jewish children were barred from non-Jewish schools. In 1939, Jews were forced to hand in all possessions made of gold or silver, lost their rights as tenants, and were disallowed the opportunity to hold government jobs. They were no longer allowed outside after nine p.m., and were told they couldn't own radio sets. In November 1939, Jews had to begin to wear yellow stars on their clothing. By 1941, many German Jews were ordered into forced labor. The establishment of ghettos, labor and death camps, and the organization of killing squads subsequently killed off millions.

Jacob Baruch

What good is a lifted finger against a lifted machine gun?

Jews who resisted Hitler's commands were targeted for punishment. If they managed to escape before it was doled out, their friends and members of their community might be punished in their stead. This knowledge, plus the lack of guns and lack of military training, discouraged Jews from fighting back.

Bessie Katz

The first time it happened I was six—
Much too young to understand,
And much too small to stop Him.
I could do nothing, not even scream,
For his hand was heavy across my mouth
And his threats were loud in my ears.

The next time He came I feigned sleep.
Limp as a rag doll, I lay.
Then the stirrings began...
A gentle vibration beneath my ribs
That rose to my throat, to my head,
Until I burst free of my body!

Below, He grunted and heaved.
But floating effortlessly above the bed,
I was removed from the pain.
Years later, in the camp,
When life seemed too ugly to bear,
I would remember...and fly!

Was I in the Stutthof concentration camp?
Upon occasion.

In many cases a prisoner's survival in concentration camps depended upon both luck and quickly-honed survival skills. They learned to barter possessions for extra food, to become inconspicuous, and to snare choice work assignments. Their desire to live was nurtured by religious and spiritual beliefs, anger, plans for escape, concern for family members, and a sense of responsibility that they must survive in order to share their stories. Bessie Katz (in this poem) removed herself from the horrors through a technique called an "out of body experience." Abused children sometimes talk about learning to "leave their bodies" during assaults, thereby disconnecting them from the events.

Irony

(Young German Soldier)

Born to tears of joy
Buried without mourners' tears
Born to welcoming prayers
Buried sans last rites
Born and bred to lead
Buried following an idiot's order
Born to satin and velvet
Buried in an unlined box
Born to carry on the family name
Buried in a nameless grave
Born to onyx and marble
Buried without the meanest sandstone marker
Born to live
Buried

Gossip Mill

Did you Hear?
They still haven't found Gala's girl...missing since last
Friday!
She's ruined for sure. I heard it said she ran off with the
tailor's son—
The Jew boy? Had his way with her? Better at the bottom
of the well, I say!
Better in the well than damned to hell, I say!
Amen

Did you Hear?
Elka's best egg layer disappeared right out of the coop!
Damn tinker-dicker man snatched it for sure.
Those greedy Jews would steal your soul if you left it
laying about, I say!
Better a leaky roof than an empty larder, I say!
Amen

Did you Hear?
Dosha's boy's gone touched. He's lost his mind...babbling
like a fool.
Scared out of his senses, I say. Must have seen something
awful!

...Well, (They're making that matzah again—a cup of flour
and some Christian blood...)
Better a daft boy than a dead one, I say!
Amen

Did you Hear?
I was up all night. Who could sleep with that baby wailing?
Unnatural!
They're at it again, I say! Sacrificing children left and right.
Of course they've been doing it since time began—used to
feed their own to Moloch.
Better their own than ours, I say!
Amen

Did you Hear?
They're rounding up the Jews. Good riddance, I say!
God Almighty, help Hitler rid the world of those rapists
and thieves,
Exterminate the rodents, the vermin, I pray!
No better than they deserve, I say!
Amen

Matzah is unleavened bread eaten during the Jewish Passover
holiday. The food reminds Jews of a time when, fleeing from
slavery, their ancestors had no time to allow their bread to rise.
The exodus, under the guidance of Moses, was the first leg on
their journey to the Promised Land.

Moloch was the Sun God, believed to have been worshiped by
the ancient Canaanites. Firstborn children were sacrificed to the
deity in a bizarre ceremony during which the child was placed in
the arms of the bronze idol filled with fire. The arms could then
be lifted to the idol's mouth so that the child fell through into
the flames within.

Stasi Oppenheiner

We are born to die
And no great tragedy in that!
For no flame burns forever
And most shed so little light
That those beyond its immediate pool
Scarce notice when the insignificant thing is snuffed.

But when one who is born
With exceptional talent and promise
Is removed before fulfilling her destiny—
That, then, is truly tragic.
So, while I did not lament my fate,
I fretted mightily over my friend, Annes.

I prayed she would live to see the war's end—
Live to write our story,
So the world might hear, and remember,
The deeds of evil men
And how we suffered at their hands.

But more so, how we fought
Fear and despair to the end,
Clinging to hope and to each other,

Kerry Arquette

As we strove to believe
In the ultimate power of good over evil!

Anne Frank was born in Germany in 1929, but spent most of her short life in the Netherlands. When, in 1942, Anne's family was ordered to report for deportation, they moved secretly into the annex of one of Otto Frank's businesses. There, Anne, her older sister, their parents, and four others lived in cramped darkness for more than two years. During that time, Anne kept a diary detailing her life and thoughts. In 1944, the annex was raided and the residents were sent to Auschwitz. A month later, Anne and her sister were transported to Bergen-Belsen. They died of typhus in 1945, only weeks before liberation. Anne's father, the family's sole survivor, later found and published Anne's diary.

Corporal Thomas Smyth

(British Prisoner of War)

Over the wire
On a folding ladder
Made of rickety wood,
Stored, until the moment's hour
In plain sight of the enemy
As a barrack bookshelf.
My bridge to freedom.

Captured two days later.

Through the gate
Disguised as a woman,
A camp whore.
Stopped and questioned
By the lusty gate guard
Whose pawing hand
Shifted a false bosom.

Captured immediately.

Kerry Arquette

Under the wire,
Through a dark tunnel,
Voices hushed, muffled pants,
Knuckles bleeding,
Crawling forward, up, out—
Cool air on my heated face,
Stooped, running free.

Captured two weeks later.

"*Fur Sie ist der Krieg vorbei!*"
"For you the war is over!"
Sent to a camp for incorrigibles
Grinning like a fool
Planning my next escape
Knowing this game may kill me
Knowing it's what keeps me alive.

Out of an estimated fifteen million men and a few women who were WWII prisoners of war, six million did not survive. Despite rules outlined in the Geneva Convention (signed in 1929 by forty-seven nations) that dictated humane treatment of prisoners, many of those who were captured suffered terribly. Even those who were not tortured, starved, or overworked were overcome with mental anguish and isolation. Boredom was one of the prisoner's most debilitating enemies. Escape plans helped pass the time, occupy a soldier's mind, and keep up his spirits.

Timothy Robbins

Jack isn't as scarded of giants as me
Cause he got away.
He slided down the beanstalk and chopped it up to bits.
Then the giant's butt hit the ground Hard!
Hah!

David isn't worried of giants either.
He was good at slingshotting
And he bonked Goliath in the head with a rock,
And the giant died and David won.
Yeah!

If I was a brave giant killer I probly wouldn't cry
When the sky splits open with lightening rain,
And big smashing feet wobble my house.
Boom, Boom, Boom!
BOOM!

My...I...then, there's no air 'cause the giant sucks it all in.
And I shake and my hands are sticky, drippy,
So I crawl under my bed to lie flat as...as...
And I close my eyes and stick pointer fingers in my ears.
Disappeared.

From far off I hear'd Mama screaming.
"Timmy, Oh, God! Tim, WHERE ARE YOU?"
Somethin' was wailing and the stomps bammed
And no way, *noooo way*, was I going to come out—
Ever.

The first major German air raid in London took place in the evening of September 7, 1940. Bombers destroyed large portions of the less-affluent East End. Londoners who were initially terrified of the attack soon became accustomed to the nightly raids. At the sound of the bomb sirens, they would routinely move to basement shelters and underground subway platforms. While the shelters offered some protection, most could not stand up to a direct hit. Those who survived the raids sometimes emerged to find their houses leveled.

Hannah Deutchman

Housed in unheated structures
Fed rancid table scraps
Forced to scrounge for garbage pail bones
Branded like livestock
Herded by dogs
Expected to respond to commands
Put outside in all weather
Subjected to kicks and beatings
Mounted and ridden
Separated from babies
Infested, itching, and oozing
Experimented upon to "further science"
Put down

Treated like an animal,
I became an animal,
Ripping at the guard's throat
With my nails and teeth,
Then howling my kill
As the hunter's bullet found its mark.

Not all prisoners of Hitler's death camps went quietly to the gas chambers. There are documented cases of large organized prisoner uprisings in the death camps of Treblinka, Sobibor, and Auschwitz-Birkenau. Additionally, smaller groups of prisoners as well as individuals are also known to have fought back. Many escape attempts took place while prisoners were outside the camp wire on work details. In 1942, Meir Berliner, a Jewish prisoner at Treblinka whose wife and daughter had been gassed, stabbed to death a guard. Berliner was killed immediately. One hundred fifty prisoners were killed the next day as punishment for Berliner's act.

Christine Soloman

They posed as pious,
But gossiped behind wagging fingers,
Lusted for each other's husbands,
And envied their neighbors' gains.

They posed as pious,
But turned on Jewish neighbors,
Pointing fingers and naming names,
Then claiming abandoned treasures.

They posed as pious,
Scorning me, the village whore.
But I alone hid innocents—
Sharing my room and meager fare.

They posed as pious,
Flocking to watch as bullets riddled
The body so many had enjoyed,
While crowing about the wages of sin.

They posed as pious,
Yet my body lies gently and my soul soars;
Deeds judged by higher, holier powers,
Who ushered me, alone, through heaven's gates.

Among the righteous were individuals and communities who refused to hand their Jewish neighbors over to the Nazis for deportation and execution and those who gave refuge in basements, attics, homes, barns, churches, and orphanages. The reward for turning Jews over to authorities was a quart of liquor, four pounds of sugar, a carton of cigarettes or, perhaps, a small amount of money. The penalty for hiding Jews was death.

Ivan Romarov

From the Source we flowed,
Two separate life bodies,
Gurgling, trilling, swirling
Around obstacles, bound toward
A compelling unknown.
Gaining momentum, our souls
Merged in an explosive concussion,
And we became one
Driving force that swept past
Social prejudice and family pressures.
Our thundering hearts
Drowned out strident protests
That Jews and Christians *mustn't.*
And Nazi rantings
Could no more separate us
Than could their bellows
Cleave the ocean.
When ordered apart,
We tossed our heads
And slipped to our loving place
To embrace the path of least resistance.
Together, we flowed back to the Source.

The Nuremberg Laws were passed by the Nazi Party on September 15, 1935. They included the *Gesetz zum Schutze des deutschen Blutes und der deutshen Ehre* (Law to Protect German Blood and German Honor), also known as *Blutschutzgesetz*. The law forbade marriage and sexual relationships between Jews and non-Jews, as well as relations between Germans and the "Romani people" or "Afro-Germans."

Valeriy Romarov

(Ivan Romarov's Christian Wife)

There used to be a sandy trail,
That snaked its way across this land.
When we were young, and quite in love,
We'd walk that pathway hand in hand.

There used to be a lemon tree,
And once there was a rushing stream.
When we were young, and quite in love,
We'd sit upon its bank and dream.

We'd lie upon this grassy hill,
And sleep together in the glen,
Where now we spend eternity...

So much has changed—
And naught has changed—
Since then.

Bernard Zahlerova

"Sissy, Sissy,
Go away.
Don't come back,
Another day."

Vicious Children,
Stuck in time,
Taunting classmates
With cruel rhyme.

"Filthy, Faggot,
Stupid queer,
Kiss the boy,
You hold so dear."

Bullies, Bullies,
Almost grown,
Hand still clutching
Stick and stone.

"Stinking, Pervert,
In our town.
Round him up,
To put him down."

Loveless Soldiers
Made of tin,
Hearts attuned
To hatred's din.

"Homo, Homo,
Marked with pink.
Die and rid us
Of your stink."

Nazi Killers
Spare the rod,
We are all
The Sons of God.

Homosexuality was a crime in Nazi Germany. Identified through their memberships in homosexual organizations and attendance at known homosexual clubs and other hangouts, homosexual men and women were hunted down and arrested by the Gestapo. Homosexual males were sometimes freed if they agreed to be castrated. Those refusing this option were sent to concentration camps where, by 1942, all imprisoned homosexuals were forcibly castrated. Fewer lesbians than male homosexuals were arrested during the war years, but those who were imprisoned were often raped and used as prostitutes by soldiers and guards. Homosexuals in concentration camps were identified by pink triangles stitched to their clothes. An estimated one hundred thousand to one million homosexuals were killed by Nazis during the war.

Zarko Jenische

Dance, Roma, dance!

In the fields and forests we danced,
Skirts a swirling blaze and patched boots stomping
To the rhythm, to-the-bone, to-the-soul.
Stone-bare chests, glazed with sweat, heaved
While heavy bosoms rolled and swayed.
Eyes closed, spreading inky lashes on mocha cheeks,
Eyes opened, spreading taunting invitations for shared
lust.
Lips drawn back in angelic smiles, devilish grimaces
Flashed teeth that glinted as they caught the firelight.
The perfume of dust and life hard-earned,
Hard-lived, hard-loved, hovered over the Gypsy camp.

In the fields and forests we sang,
Instruments cradled like coddled babes in sinewy arms,
Fingertips slipping, pressing, plucking.
Voices soared on night winds, moon-baying melodies that,
Filled the soul and confused our empty bellies.
Ancient lyrics, unknown, unspoken by *gadje'*,
Recalled centuries of our oppression and torment.
Hunted and murdered across time and territory,

We savored the spark, the flames, the smoke and cinders
of life,
Knowing that lurking just outside our clearing
The wolves gathered, once again, for the *Porrajmos*—
"devouring."

Dance Roma, dance!

Gadje' is the term used by Romani (Gypsy) people for non-
Romas.

Porrajmos is the Romani word for the Holocaust. Translated, it
means, "the devouring."

Roma, commonly called Gypsies, were one of the groups
targeted by the Nazis for extermination. Long before Hitler
came to power, the Romani were persecuted because of their
dark complexions and refusal to conform to local religious and
social norms. In Hitler's Germany, Romas were rounded up for
deportation, imprisonment, forced labor, and sterilization. In
January 1940, two hundred fifty Romani children were used to
test Zyklon-B gas. Thousands of Romas were gunned down by
SS death squads in the forests and countryside. Others were sent
to concentration camps where they wore a black triangle on their
clothes, representing those imprisoned for anti-social behavior.
The letter "Z" was tattooed on their arms. It is believed that
between one-half and one and a half million Romas were
murdered during WWII.

Esmerelda Jenische

(Zarko Jenische's Daughter)

Our life was
Filled with a wild joy and abandon They could never
understand,
Only envy.
Filled with a nomad's freedom They could never
understand,
Only envy.
Filled with soul-soaring music and movement They could
never understand,
Only envy.
Filled with fire and heat and passion They could never
understand,
Only envy.
Filled with risk and excitement They could never
understand.
Only envy.

No wonder They hated us so.

Hilda Wolf

Behind my tiny, tidy house,
Within the picket fenced-in yard,
Beneath the rich and fertile soil,
I planted many lovely things,
Like turnips, onions, carbine rifles,
Oiled pouches filled with maps,
A bin of vouchers to buy food
For hungry, frightened, hidden Jews.

Behind my crepey, wrinkled face,
Beneath my white-haired, tidy bun,
Inside my nodding, bobbing head,
I stored the many facts I heard
When soldiers' mouths began to wag,
Not guessing that a sweet-faced crone
Would understand the plans they made,
And hand them on to allied knights.

Inside my lovely, little house,
Within my spare and lonely room,
Behind my bony, blue-veined hand,
I giggled like a teenage girl
At all the strutting, silly fools who

Kerry Arquette

Think the biggest, brightest box
Is sure to hold the diamond ring,
And covers tell a volume's worth.

Eero Kauranen

(Finnish Soldier)

I was your worst nightmare,
A ghostly apparition
Conjured from swirling snow.
Dressed all in white,
Faceless, formless against the drifts,
I simply appeared—a demon,
Satan-sent to snatch up those
Whose murderous, sinning souls
Would fail judgment,
And carry them to Hell.

Descending like unearthly mist,
I watched your eyes widen
Above a silent scream.
My blade found your throat,
And you struggled to genuflect—
A last-ditch flailing, failing plea
For holy absolution.
Like your victims, you died in terror.
They say fear is worst than death...
Is it true?

In November 1939, the Soviets invaded Finland. Believing the Scandinavian country would easily fall to their overwhelmingly superior military strength, the Soviets were surprised at how fervently the Finns fought back. Although outnumbered and under-armed, the Finns could claim some advantages: Unlike the Russians, they were familiar with the rugged terrain and hostile weather of their native turf, and they were at home on skis. Dressed all in white, they could traverse the difficult landscape, silently sneaking up and attacking Russian troops. Many Finns were also excellent huntsmen and, therefore crack shots. Despite these strengths, the Finns were destined to lose. With their ammunition and manpower depleted, they finally surrendered in March 1940. The campaign, known as the "Winter War" claimed twenty-five thousand Finnish lives and another forty-three thousand were wounded.

Kesar Radogost

(Russian Soldier Killed By Eero Kauranen)

Buried to my waist in drifts, I trudged
On feet gone mercifully numb.
With fingers too frozen to feel,
I rubbed eyes burned and too weary to see.
Later, starving and lightheaded,
I huddled in an icy hole trying to sleep,
Then, from heaven, an angel appeared,
Silent, shimmering, white—so white.
My damaged eyes gaped and
My mouth opened to praise God's name,
But a searing in my throat cut short my words.
Arms clumsy with cold, I signed my faith,
For just as I had given Him my life,
I would joyfully trust Him with my death.
Praise the Lord! Praise the Lord
For sustaining me through my trials and
Sending His divine messenger
To deliver me from my frozen misery
Into His warm embrace.

During the "Winter War" fought on Finnish territory during the winter of 1939-1940, the Soviets lost two hundred thousand soldiers. At least another three hundred thousand were wounded before the campaign was done. Russian soldiers who did not fall to Finnish bullets often starved or froze to death when Finnish troops adeptly divided the invading lines, cutting pods of Russian soldiers off from food and supplies. The bodies of many of these fallen men weren't discovered until after the spring thaw.

Gustav Moller

Born a Dane,
I was chased by Death to a thriving port
Then hidden in the womb of a fishing boat.
I lay for hours in the dark, warm, damp,
As the vessel beneath me swayed
To the swooshing tune of a sea lullaby.
Hushed murmurs and a heartbeat pressed close,
So I did not, *could not* move.
Until I heard my mother's urgent cry.
Then, came pain and pressure as she pushed me
Toward the light, into fresh air and freedom.
I stretched my cramped legs
And wailed at the unfamiliar world.
For, by the hand of God, and a brave skipper,
I had been reborn in Sweden.

When the Nazis invaded Denmark in 1940, they met little resistance. In fact, the Danes suffered the German troops' presence with behavior bordering on cordial. But in 1943, when Hitler ordered the evacuation of Denmark's seven thousand five hundred to eight thousand Jews to the labor camp of Theresienstadt, Czechoslovakia, the Danes mounted a campaign unprecedented in the war. Immediately after receiving word of the Nazis' plans, the Danes began hiding their Jewish neighbors and friends. Jews were then smuggled to ports, where fishing boats ferried them to neutral Sweden. Although four hundred eighty-one Jews were captured, most reached safe shores. Applying unrelenting pressure on the Nazis, the Danes made sure most of those who had been captured survived their confinement.

Thomas Jensen

(Captain of the Boat That Ferried Gustav Moller to Sweden)

Through stinging spray of salt and sea,
My eyes were set on the distant shore,
Where cloud and wave and land did meet.
Though the sleet did fall and the rains did pour,
The thrill of the hunt enveloped me.

Riding low with my damp hull crammed
With trusting souls who were forced to flee
From the spidered flags that snapped and whipped
And rose and dipped to their Lord's decree.
The waves hid the cries of the wailing damned.

With shark-like stealth It cut the mist,
A slate gray cold and ghostly ship.
Like death beneath a lifeless sky.
But on steered I with a bloodless grip.

Kerry Arquette

As the night closed in, I raised my fist,
And grinned to hear their hue and cry,
For I had bigger fish to fry.

An estimated seventy fishing boats carried Denmark's Jews across two miles of the North Sea to Sweden. Unlike Jews in other occupied countries, Danish Jews who returned to their homeland after the war found their houses and possessions waiting for them, their yards tended and their pets cared for.

Hana Voigt

The paved streets writhed with flames;
A sea of licking, blue-tongued serpents,
And the inferno roared like Dante's demons.
But we could not stay in the basement shelter
Where the smoky air was poisoned with gas,
So we surged up the steps toward Hell,
Where swirling fires obscured all—all
But the charred, shrunken bodies of neighbors,
And the screaming, gaily bedecked circus horses,
That bucked, galloping frantically in circles,
And the sight of panic-stricken mothers
Pushing baby strollers blindly into the flames.

With a whip and a scream, a blistering tornado
Tore up an ancient tree by its roots, sucked up a roof,
Then ripped the baby basket from my arms,
And my sobbing toddler's hand from my grasp,
Pitching them against a building which crumpled
Upon their broken bodies like a child's block tower.
The plastic handle of my purse exploded
And my wedding ring and its finger were gone!
My nylons melted like boiled sugar against my skin.
The fillings in my teeth turned poker-hot.

I screamed, as heat hit nerves... just moments before
My hair burst into a halo of orange flame.

By February 13, 1945, the war was winding down. Germany's defeat was in sight and the German town of Dresden, a center of art and leisure, swelled with refugees fleeing from the allied thrust. The people of Dresden were caught unaware by the Royal Air Force air attack that brought death to between one hundred and three hundred thousand, and destroyed much of the city. During the initial stages of the attack, British planes dropped more than three thousand four hundred tons of bombs and incendiary devices on the center of town. The bombs and a strong wind created a firestorm, a tornado of fire, that swept up or incinerated everything in the vicinity. Those who survived recalled, how horses freed from the resident circus, galloped madly through the flames. Survivors found themselves at the mercy of American fighters that attacked the next day, shooting any living target. Because of the timing of the attack and the fact that Dresden was not a German military stronghold nor the producer of military products, many viewed the bombing as an immoral and unnecessary aggressive act against civilians.

Chaya Shulamit

Passion left on a train to Sobibor.
Love disappeared into a toddler-filled grave.
Home went to greedy neighbors.
Art departed into Nazi bunkers.
Wine vanished into the bellies of SS soldiers.
Song ran to silence.
Faith evaporated.
Hope fled.
I saw no reason to stay.

While experts estimate the number of victims who died in Nazi extermination and work camps, it is unknown how many people, consumed by despair and overwhelmed by their losses, took their own lives during or immediately after the war.

Rosa Dekel

Dying is a sigh
Soft as the kiss of a butterfly's wing,
Light as mist on your tongue.
Dying is the tinkling silence
Of a wind chime a hundred miles a way.
It is the warmed golden beach sand
Beneath your knees and neck.
Dying is the gurgle of love
That rises in your throat
When your child giggles.
It is the lifting of your heart
As the breeze's fingers ruffle your hair
And the perfume of flowers tickles a memory
Of magic, anything-could-happen springs.
Dying is that moment when
The sunset's red and orange
Flashes green, before fading to black.

After all I endured,
Dying was lovely,
And, oh,
So very
easy.

Kerry Arquette

Elsbeth Dekel

Mama said dying is like jumping into a cold pond—
You take a deep breath, one big step, and then SPLASH!
You really only have to be brave for a moment,
And before you know it, the shock is over.

Mama said dying only takes a moment.
But in Auschwitz, dying begins when hope disappears;
When the Selected are boarded into their barracks.
And you know, you *know, you know*!

Later, after nightfall, you march to the showers
Beneath chimneys spewing human flames.
The ashes of other girls land on your hair and you wonder,
Do *they* know they are these black snowflakes?

Stepping in dusty footprints of those who passed before,
Fear rises in your throat, strangling, choking.
Sternly you tell yourself, "If others survived this, so can I."
Only to realize that they...didn't...

Your mind struggles to grasp what can't be understood.
You plead, making deals with a God
You no longer believe in, but promise to embrace if only...

If only He will intervene.

At the showers you are forced to undress,
Then shoved into a room, bare, cold as a tomb
And built so tight not even angels can hear
The weeping that echoes off the gray walls.

Through terror-glazed eyes you watch your death-mates
Curl into fetal positions or glare defiant as Maccabee
warriors.
Old women pray, friends embrace, mothers weave golden
pictures
Of a heaven where they and their children shall meet.
From the depth of your soul you cry out,
"I want my Mommy!"

The hiss of gas...

I can't be dead!
I don't want to be dead!
I don't know *how* to be dead!

Oh God, oh God, I'll hold my breath, Oh God!!!!!

Mama was wrong.
In Hitler's camps dying takes *forever*.

Hana Rosenmayer

If he'd had dripping fangs or talon-like claws,
Or had his hair wriggled with slugs and worms,
His eyes glowed red and his mouth smelled like rotting
corpses,
Would I have climbed on his lap, clamoring for his
attention?

If his hands had been stained blood red,
His pockets been filled with snakes and people-parts,
If his laugh had prickled my neck like a werewolf's howl,
Would I have swung gaily across the camp holding his
gloved hand?

If he had, even once, shown me the monster
That lurked beneath the angel trappings
Would I have stuck hopeful fingers into the pockets of his
SS uniform,
Looking for the treats he often hid there?

Would I have gone, terrified, but willingly, with him to the
labs?

Would I have believed his promises that he would never,
ever hurt me?

Would I have been prepared for the injections, the slicing,
and maiming?

Would I have loved him despite it all?

Dr. Josef Mengele was responsible for a number of duties at Auschwitz. Not only did he meet arriving trains, he determined with a flick of a finger which of the new prisoners would live and which would die immediately. Many survivors carry strong memories of Mengele, always impeccably dressed and groomed, always smiling, looking more like a movie star than your average doctor. When not involved in the selections, Mengele immersed himself in barbaric medical studies. His favorite subjects had dwarfism, giantism, or were sets of twins. Mengele saw twins as the perfect guinea pigs for genetic studies. He is said to have sewn twins together in an attempt to produce Siamese twins, injected their eyes to try to change their color, and often castrated and maimed them. Of the three thousand twins Mengele experimented upon, fewer than ten percent are believed to have survived. Despite the suffering inflicted on them, many of the twins reportedly liked "Uncle Mengele," who could be exceedingly charming and projected the image of a caring relative.

Karoline Rosenmayer

(Hana Rosenmayer's Twin Sister)

Mama said, "I'll meet you two at the gates."
But she wasn't there on Monday.
She wasn't there on Tuesday.
She wasn't there on Wednesday.
She wasn't there that week at all,
Or the next week or the next month.
That winter, she never appeared,
Though I looked for her during roll call.
And she wasn't there in the spring when
They marched Hana and me to the labs
For the Bad Things to happen.
Mama wasn't at the gates in the summer,
When the twins were allowed out
To pick wild flower bouquets.
But, in the fall Hana died and then,
Finally, God called me home as well.
And there at the gates waited Mama
Wearing her best I-love-you face,
And her arms opened to fold me up.
"I told you I'd be here my darling!"

When trains arrived as Auschwitz, Dr. Josef Mengele was there to meet the prisoners. He made immediate determinations based upon age, health, and labor needs as to which prisoners should be gassed immediately and which should be kept alive for a bit longer. Mengele was always on the lookout for twins to use in his gruesome experiments. After separating the twins from their parents, they were taken to a separate barrack near the crematorium. As Mengele's twins, they had a certain status within the camp population. Mengele made sure that his twins were exempt from the daily selections. They were better fed than other prisoners. Unlike the rest of the prison population, the twins were not shorn of their hair. Mengele even arranged for them to receive some form of recreation—the boys played soccer and the girls were taken on outings to collect wildflowers. Unfortunately, most of the twins used in Mengele's labs perished.

Alessandro D'Addezio

My grave is cold
But my heart burns with pride,
For I,
A cheat,
A liar,
A petty thief,
A plagiarizer,
An adulterer,
A coveter in life,
Saved one Jew.

Violette Stein

Hope
Held my hand
As I walked to the train.
Hope
Waved goodbye
When I left home behind.
Hope
Hovered, a memory shadow,
Outside the wire.
Hope
Smiled trustingly, innocently,
In my dreams.
Hope
Gave me the courage
To face my loathsome task.
Hope
Made me sort the dead Jews' clothes
For it kept me alive.
Hope
Vanished when I pulled
One tiny jacket from the heaps.
"Hope"
Read the name inside the collar—

Stitched with my best hand.
Hope
I knew, Oh God, *I knew*,
Was gone forever.
And a world without Hope,
A world without my baby,
Was a world I simply couldn't face.

Some prisoners in the death camps were spared immediate gassing in order to provide labor. Often, these selected few were assigned the task of carting bodies, cleaning out the gas chambers, pulling teeth from corpses for their gold fillings, and sorting and readying clothes of dead Jews. These clothes, left on hooks outside the gas chambers when the prisoners were ordered to undress in readiness for "showers," were sent to needy Aryan Germans.

Lia Kumosa

Only the choicest blossoms were plucked,
Stem, leaves, and glorious yellow blooms
Wrenched from their roots
By coarse and greedy hands.
The flowers of my life, my Natan and Tsila,
Bruised, dewy tears streaking,
Tossed into a market wagon.
Off to decorate the homes of Aryans.

Planted in love, grown in my belly,
Fed by my blood and breasts,
Coaxed, trained, guided,
Pruned religiously as needed,
But never coddled nor spoiled,
So that they might rise toward the sun,
So that they might see a future, a world,
Far beyond my view.

Arms outstretched, they beseeched,
"Mama, Mama, help!"
But what could I do?
Scream, weep, and fuel their terror?
Attack, and take bullets before their eyes?

Throw myself beneath the wagon's wheels
So they might see my bloodied body
Over their shoulders?

No, there was nothing I could do
For these blooms for whom I would do anything.
So I sucked my tongue
And sent them off with a cluck and a wave,
Admonishments to stand up straight.
Then I turned to meet my inevitable fate.
Laid to rest in a muddy puddle.
No flowers marked my passing.

In order to increase their population, Nazis kidnapped "Aryan looking," children (including an estimated fifty thousand Poles) from occupied countries so that they might be raised by German families as "good Germans." Many of these were later cast out by their adoptive parents and ended up dying of disease or starvation. Although efforts were made by numerous organizations after the war to reunite parents with their children, many children were never found. Their fates are unknown.

Natan Kumosa

(Lia Kumosa's Son)

I fought until sweaty to prove a point.
I fought until bruised to avenge an insult.
I fought until bloody to defend a weaker kid.
I fought until broken to keep what's mine.
If I were a parent,
I would have fought until dead to save my children.
My moth—that *woman* did nothing at all!

Tsila Kumosa

(Lia Kumosa's Daughter)

S-s-s-sometimes it's h-h-hard
T-to s-s-say w-w-what y-you w-w-ant.
But the more you p-p-ractice
The easier it g-gets.
I can talk t-to my doll, Maryanne,
With n-n-no s-stutter at all.
M-maybe M-mama sh-should have p-practiced m-more.
Then her m-mouth could have s-poken
What her eyes w-were sh-shouting—
"I l-l-love you."

Saul Markiewicz

No pain
No fear
Hope, hunger, longing,
Empty-eyed
Empty sack
Human rag
Boneless, filthy, formless, gray
Crumpled
Worthless
No thought of here
Or there
Too worn to move
Too *nothing* to be moved
Mouth dry—tongue stuck
Head gourd-heavy, heavy
Fingers, rat food
Don't care
Waiti*ng*
Waiti*in*
Wa*iti*
W*ait*
W*ai*
W*a*

W

Dear G-d,
Hear my prayer.
Those who step over my pitiful form
Whisper bitterly about Your neglect.
"How could He," they ask,
"Turn His back on the muselmann—living dead?"
I have not the energy nor will to explain
What tomorrow or next week or next month
They will come to understand on their own.
How great is your compassion, G-d,
That you would send this balm of
Numbing indifference
To anesthetize me
When I could simply bear
No more.

Life for prisoners in Hitler's labor and death camps was unbearable. Starved, beaten, traumatized, ill, lonely, grieving, shocked, and lost, many became severely depressed. They withdrew from activities, stopped eating and communicating. These souls were called "Muselmann," or living dead. Unable to work, they were shot or gassed.

Juta Benicoeur

(Kappo)

She, the village scour woman,
Knees crusted and tough as elephant skin,
Lye-leathered from washing floors.
"Clean this. Scrub that," the Jews ordered Mami.
And she, bent-backed and beaten down,
Knelt before them to do their bidding
For pittance—becoming such a pitiable object
That none in our town nodded good day,
But sniffed instead, and turned aside.
No tea invitations, no social calls came her way.
She, a tattered woman, old before her time,
Who asked for so little and was given less.

He, the village tinker-dicker man,
In twice-turned shirt and twine-belted pants,
Blackened palms, nail-filled mouth, hammer at ready,
Was worth a nod and a passing hello.
For they never knew when Papa's able hands
Might be needed to hang a door or patch a roof.
But no spot was held on the sun-warmed bench

Kerry Arquette

Where the men gathered to speak of things
No tinker-dicker man would understand—
Or so they thought. And no one saved him a seat
Near the eastern wall during morning Shma.

Me, that lumbering boy with the pock-marked face
And rotting teeth and sour breathe.
Teased and scorned, beaten to tears and rages
That bode ill for the stray cat found disemboweled
On the schoolhouse steps, or the flaming rat hung
Candle-like from the park tree on Chanukah night.
Prayers for justice oozed like puss from boyhood wounds,
And prayers were answered when the Nazis
Made me a camp Kappo—overseer of other Jews.
With their nod and a rod, I found my vengeance,
Stoking fires of misery until my former classmates and
neighbors
Experienced the kind of Hell I called home.

Shma is the name of an important Jewish prayer.

The Kappos were inmates assigned the job of overseeing fellow
prisoners in Hitler's camps. Often hardened criminals, they were
notorious for mistreating those under their watch, doling out
beatings and other punishments at whim. The Kappo
tormentors were viewed as traitors by fellow prisoners and were
often more hated than the Nazi guards. Some Kappos were
attacked or murdered by infuriated prisoners.

Itzik Falk

Over our shoulder was home.
Down the street, around the corner, across the field,
and mountain and water,
Beyond memory, ensconced in history, and legend,
and lore,
There was a place where Jews could thrive and live,
and live.
But we could not go there.

So we wandered the world,
Nomads, pausing to build businesses, schools, and schules,
And strength and dreams—before being driven out.
And those structures crumbled to brick and stone,
That paved the way toward a place, we prayed, we could
call our own.

We stopped by the hundreds, the thousands, in Germany,
Where we dug in and raised up houses of sweat and heart,
And hope that we might rest in peace until traveling on.
We came to believe, falsely, that our foundations were
strong enough
To survive the howl of prejudice, the winds of politics.

We watched in shocked impotence as our walls crumbled.
Once again at the mercy of the elements, too shocked
to run,
We stood exposed and vulnerable to the hatred
that whirled,
Destroying all that we had built, snatching us from
our plots,
And setting us down in camps of hunger, pain, and gas.

And with our last dying breath
From that place inside that aches with a longing bordering
on pain,
We cried out like lost children to the G-d of Abraham,
Isaac, and Jacob.
And those who recalled His promises,
left this world believing
They would reopen their eyes in Palestine.
Home, at last.

The *Galut* (Diaspora) was the dispersion of the Jewish people during the sixth and eighth century BCE out of the Levant and Palestine, and into the largely non-Jewish countries of North Africa and Europe. Jewish exiles formed large and insular communities in most major cities, often living peacefully alongside Gentile neighbors for long stretches of time. However, in almost every country where Jews found refuge, periodic outbreaks of latent anti-Semitism triggered pograms, Inquisitions, and other forms of violent persecution, repeatedly forcing Jews to abandon their adoptive homes and seek new sanctuaries. Flight, refuge, settlement, assault, flight: the pattern repeated for centuries. But by the early twentieth century, the cycle had slowed; robust Jewish communities had become entrenched in the businesses, governments, and academic circles of major European cities. While nominally espousing or supporting fringe Zionist efforts to develop a Jewish homeland in the Middle East, many prominent members of the Jewish community believed that after more than 2,000 years living in Europe, cities like Berlin, Paris, Prague, Warsaw, and Vienna were the Jews' home.

Fela Daum

(Age 5)

We gotted off the train and they tooked our clothes
And then they sented us to the Wasp Place.
A witch lady grabbed my arm and said mean, "Hold still!"
Mama closed my eyes so I couldn't see and then
A million trillion wasps started to sting and sting my wrist!
And I screamed and cried,
And Mama yelled for them to stopt but they bited more
'Til I throwed up and fell down.
When I woked up I saw the sting holes on my wrist,
Like brown poop squiggles
All red and swelled up, and Mama said,
"Leave the tattoo 'lone, my little heart," but I couldn't.
Ugly! Ugly! Off! I don't want no poopy wrist!
So I scratched it with my fingernails
But it wouldn't come clean—just bleeded.
So I scraped it in the dirt outside more and more
But it wouldn't come off—just bleeded green sticky.
"Leave it 'lone, my little love," said Mama.
But at night, when she was sleep,
I rubbed and rubbed it 'gainst my bed.

Kerry Arquette

It hurted, but I kept rubbing
'til a nail comed lose and scratched me.
Then I leaved it 'lone, but it was too late.
That nail had tetanus and so didded me.

Not all prisoners in Hitler's concentration and death camps were tattooed. However, in camps where tattooing was routine, arriving prisoners were stripped, shorn of all hair, and marched to a building where the process was performed. Survivors recall the experience as being both painful and traumatizing. The numbers, often burned into the inside of the left forearm, were a way of identifying both the prisoner's "crime" and served as a method of identification which made it easier for camp officials to select prisoners for extermination, work details, and deportation to other camps.

Elka Dajbog

God knows what is in every person's mind and heart,
right?
So, if I denounced my faith but did not *mean* it,
He would know. Wouldn't He?
He would *know* that the words I spoke to appease the
Nazis weren't true.
And so, wouldn't it be better to mouth hollow words
denying His presence
Than to proclaim my faith and die a martyr?
Why would God want or need another martyr?
What use is a martyr?
A martyr cannot bear witness to the Lord's power and
mercy,
Or bear children to praise His name.
A martyr cannot demonstrate the beauty of observance, of
faith.
A martyr's flame burns brightly for a moment then fades,
And the reasons he threw himself upon the pyre
Are, more often than not, forgotten.
So, sure that God would understand, I denied my religion,
Only to die of a ruptured appendix within a fortnight.
Divine retribution?

Jehovah's Witnesses were one of the groups identified by Hitler as enemies of the Nazi movement. On April 1, 1935, the religious group was legally banned. They were forbidden to produce religious literature and to congregate. Witnesses lost their jobs and were ousted from schools, beaten, and ostracized. Witnesses were given the option of renouncing their faith or facing torture or imprisonment in camps. Most refused to renounce. In concentration camps, Witnesses wore a purple triangle. About ten thousand Witnesses were imprisoned in camps and up to five thousand died.

Margherita Petacci

The crystal rested on gleaming mahogany shelves
Within carved cabinets polished silky by servants.
Behind locked doors it sat, safe from furtive hands
Intent on snatching it up to steal away.
Mine to stroke, the smooth, cool glass warmed
Beneath my fingertips, and the facets reflected
My smiling pleasure in its beauty ...until *I* was stolen.

The velvet-lined drawer groaned under the weight
Of silver platters polished to mirror-like finish.
Safe, in their dark nest from tarnish, abuse, and dents
Incurred when irresponsible servants press such treasures
Into service without regard to their delicate nature,
Abusing them like common crockery.
How *I* gloried in their metallic glow...until I was misused.

The gallery wall spilled with color and texture:
Images of landscapes, portraits, and still-lifes.
The paintings throbbed with the souls of their creators,
Who bled visions onto canvas with oil and watercolor.
In this room, protected from fire by the most methodical
planning,
Were the fruits of the world's most talented artists.

I gorged myself on their beauty...then learned that
Earthly beauty pales next to that, which lies beyond.

Upon aligning himself with Hitler, Benito Mussolini, Italy's
prime minister, adopted anti-Semitic positions. In 1938, the
Italian government passed The Racial Laws Against Jews. Laws
were passed denying Italy's small Jewish population of about
forty-seven thousand the right to marry Christian Italians, hold
top government jobs, or serve in the military. Jewish businesses
and property were confiscated. Despite intervention by the
Catholic church and private citizens who hid thousands of their
country's Jews, an estimated nine thousand Italian Jews were
arrested and sent to death camps.

Edda Vittorio

The mistress went with the Gestapo.
She couldn't take her pretties with her,
So I gathered up the sparklies and glitteries from cabinets
and drawers,
And paintings from the walls.
I traded them for food;
Bread, milk, and meat to feed my babes
So they could grow up straight and strong
And become soldiers for the Il Duce.

Il Duce was a term used for Benito Mussolini.

Mirek Sectevy

Marta thought me a special man,
And her unshakable belief made me so.
When my Marta said, "You can!" I found I *could.*
With her faith propelling and sustaining me,
I could *be* anything, *do* anything—anything at all.
So, when, with her last breath, Marta whispered,
"You can!"
I refused to give out or give in though my body
grew wasted.
Hunger gnawed holes in my belly,
And despair gnawed holes in my soul,
But I survived,
I survived!

Leningrad, Russia's former capital (then called St. Petersburg) was the home of three million people. When the city was besieged by German troops in 1941, the occupants geared up for battle. But rather than attack the city, Hitler ordered supply lines cut off and the area surrounded. With food sources closed down, those within Leningrad slowly began to starve. The people were driven to consume anything that might have life-sustaining calories, including moldy grain, sawdust, livestock feed, stinging nettles, flower bulbs, sheep-gut jelly, leaves, grass, and human flesh. Experts estimate that more than one million people died of starvation during the nine hundred day siege.

Traugott Middlestadt

That way,
The Jews plodded through the streets,
Toward filthy ghettos and crowded squalor.
Starved, weakened, diseased, many died,
And their bodies lay stacked like tinder in the gutters
Until burial could be arranged.

The other way,
The Rhine wound like a necklace of beaten silver
Along emerald green banks.
Families shared baskets overflowing with crusty bread and
spicy sausages,
While lovers shared embraces and impassioned kisses
Under a cloudless domed sky,

That way,
The Jews were driven from their hellish homes.
They were herded to train stations then loaded onto cattle
cars
Bound for bleak prison camps.
Upon arrival, they were stripped, shorn and tattooed,
Then degraded until death.

The other way,
Businesses thrived with the demands of war goods.
Deserving families moved from modest homes into
grander dwellings.
Our Aryan children learned more easily in Jew-free
classrooms.
The underbelly of society was removed,
Making the streets safer for our mothers, sisters,
and wives.

That way,
Smoke and the smell of death rose from the camps.
The skies burned red and ash drifted like snow.
Trains chugged from anywhere, *everywhere*, to the prison
gates.
Gunshots and screams broke the night's silence.
Rumors of terrible events ran rampant.

The other way,
German leaders nurtured hope and resurrected our pride,
Pointing fingers at Aryan superiority,
And affirming our natural right and responsibility to
dominate.
We came to see that today's small sacrifices were the
fertilizer
Needed to make our tomorrows bloom.

I looked the other way.

Chorus

White rabbits can be drawn from hats,
And coins plucked from ears.
Babies emerge wailing from wombs.
The deathly ill can heal and rise from their beds.
A flower often sprouts where it was never planted.
The sound of the sea can be heard in a shell.
A mountain returns your spoken words.
Fog can be seen, but never touched,
And the moon changes shape in the night sky.

The world is full of magic
And so I allow myself to believe that
Some how, some way,
Those who come after, will sense my presence,
Like a voice echoing through time.
They will pause labors or pleasures and wonder
—who?
And as long as I reside in their minds and hearts,
I will never truly be gone.

Sources

Bailey, Ronald H. and the Editors of Time-Life Books. *Prisoners of War.* Time-Life Books. Virginia. 1981

Bachrach, Susan. *Tell Them We Remember: The Story of the Holocaust.* United States Holocaust Memorial Museum. Text copyright Jeshajaha Weinbern 1994

Bethell, Nicholas and the Editors of Time-Life Books. *Russia Besieged.* Time-Life Books. Virginia. 1977

Dawidowicz, Lucy S. *A Holocaust Reader.* Behrman House, Inc. Publishers. New Jersey 1976

Elting, John R. and the Editors of Time-Life Books. *Battles For Scandinavia.* Time-Life Books. Virginia. 1981

Eman, Diet and Schaap, James. *Things We Couldn't Say.* William B. Eerdmans Publishing Company. Michigan. 1999

Frank, Anne. *Anne Frank: The Diary of a Young Girl.* New York. Bantam. 1993

Friedman, Ina R. *The Other Victims: First-person Stories of Non-Jews Persecuted by the Nazis.* Houghton Mifflin Company. Boston. 1990

Gershom, Yonassan. *Beyond the Ashes: Cases of Reincarnation from the Holocaust.* Association of Research & Enlightenment. Virginia. 1992

Gottfried, Ted. *Children of the Slaughter: Young People of the Holocaust.* Twenty-First Century Books. Connecticut. 2001

Gottfried, Ted. *Heroes of the Holocaust.* Twenty-First Century Books. Connecticut. 2001

Gottfried, Ted. *Martyrs To Madness: The Victims of the Holocaust.* Twenty-First Century Books. Connecticut. 2000

Gottfried, Ted. *Nazi Germany: The Face of Tyranny.* Twenty First Century Books. Connecticut. 2000

Greene, Joshua M. and Kumar, Shiva (Edited by) *Witness: Voices From the Holocaust.* Touchstone. New York. 2000

Henry Adams and the Editors of Time-Life Books. *Italy At War.* Time-Life Books. Virginia. 1982

Herzstein, Robert Edwin and the Editors of Time-Life Books. *The Nazis.* Time-Life Books. Virginia. 1980

Kent, Evelyn Julia and Schloss, Eva. *Eva's Story.* W.H. Allen & Company. Great Britain. 1988

Lagnado, Lucette Matalon and Dekel, Sheila Cohn. *Children of the Flames: Dr. Josef Mengele and The Untold Story of the Twins of Auschwitz.* Penguin Books. New York. 1991

Mosley, Leonard and the Editors of Time-Life Books. *Battle of Britain.* Time-Life Books. Virginia. 1977

Rogasky, Barbara. *Smoke and Ashes: The Story of the Holocaust.* Holiday House. New York. 1988

Acknowledgments

There are so many friends and family members who stood by me and supported me during the years in which I struggled to give voice to the personalities within *War Cries: Unheard Voices, Unmarked Graves*. It is impossible to name each and every one of you, but know that I know who you are and will always be grateful. When I was exhausted, emotionally wrung out, and sometimes in despair, you lifted me up and encouraged me to, once again, take my place in front of the computer.

I'd like to thank my children, Erin, Brittan, and Ryan Mahrer who summoned me back to the Light from the dark places into which each poem required delving. They were, are, and will always be my reason for living. A special thanks to Erin, whose writing and editing skills beautifully refined portions of this book. Thanks to my mother, the brilliant author Lois Duncan, who mentored me through every step of my early writing career, editing every word and phrase until I was ready to stand on my own. Thanks to my father, Don Arquette, who has never been afraid to stand up for what he believes is right and has taught me to do so as well. Thanks also to Andrea Zocchi, friend and sometimes-business partner, whose poet's soul and artist's eye helped mold the direction of the art that supports the *War Cries* poems. Andrea has always known how to deal with my "crazies" when others would throw up their hands. Special thanks to my publishers at Open Books, David Ross, and Kelly Huddleston who believe in this project and have graced it with their expertise and talent and without whose vision this book would not have come to be. Finally, thank you to my husband, Mark Senn...you make me a better woman, a better person. Because of you, I believe I am capable of most anything. With you by my side, I *know* I am.

Made in the USA
Charleston, SC
28 December 2016